YOU HAVE
PERMISSION

Developing a personal mission
beyond the walls of church.

PETE COCCO

© 2023 Pete Cocco All rights reserved. This book or any portion thereof may not be reproduced or used in any manner whatsoever without the express written permission of the publisher except for the use of brief quotations in a book review.

ISBN 979-8-35091-317-0

ENDORSEMENTS

"I am so thankful for this book. For Pete's willingness to share his life, story, and insight; from his heart to ours. Stories like these give us ideas about our own lives, they help us to believe that God is indeed with us and has a place for us in his mission."

Brian Sanders
Founder of Underground Network
Tampa FL

"Pete is an encourager and a man of integrity. He's a leader who calls the best out of people, often the kingdom potential they don't see in themselves. The 5 Part Permissions in this book are a key to enabling people to develop their own imagination, courage and practice whilst being encouraged to continually "lock arms with God" as "there really is no better way to live"

Rich Robinson
Mission strategist
Edinburgh Scotland

"This book is insightful, practical, challenging and most of all, permission-giving. If you are drowning in a sea of distraction or treading water in an ocean to maintain the status quo, this book is for you. Pete is the leader who first gave me "permission" years ago as a student athlete to dream God's dream for my life. That permission-giving dream created a ripple effect that is still rippling out to this day. I am forever grateful for this man's influence on my life."

Jon Peacock
Co-founding Pastor
Mission Church
Chicago

"This book is a rich and welcomed admonition to pursue a life of sacred intentionality and holy risk. It is a contemporary reiteration of Xavier's famous challenge to "Give up your small ambitions" and live a life that really counts, a life burning with apostolic passion. May this book ignite such fire in new generations of Jesus' followers!"

Sam Metcalf
Coordinator, Novo CoNext
Fullerton, CA

To Paulette,

My advocate, lover, and friend who makes me who I am.

You are my favorite.

CONTENTS

Part 1: Permission to Dream Big:
Developing Purposeful Direction — 1
   1. Big Source — 3
   2. Big Adventure — 12
   3. Big Scope — 19

Part 2: Permission to Be Armed and Dangerous:
Developing Holy Valor — 25
   4. Fully Armed — 27
   5. Dangerously Bright — 34

Part 3: Permission to Flip the Script:
Developing a New Sequence of Order — 55
   6. Being before Doing — 59
   7. Chaos before Order — 65
   8. Self-Discovery before Formal Teaching — 71
   9. Time before Invitation — 81
   10. Authority before Assignment — 89

Part 4: Permission to Start Fires:
Developing Contagious Aspiration — 98
   11. Fire Requires Friction — 101
   12. Fire Requires Chemistry — 115

Part 5: Permission to Prioritize Play:
Developing Creative Initiative — 127
   13. Play on a Team — 130
   14. Play Outside — 140

WE. ARE ON. A MISSION.

There was a crispness in the air, and a pit in my stomach as I rose on that sunny May morning at the end of our eighth-grade year. I was about to go to a place I'd never been, and I was more than a bit anxious. Like every class before ours, graduation from junior high was celebrated with a class trip to the biggest and baddest amusement park in the Midwest. As we approached the gates of Cedar Point, there was a buzz of excitement percolating on the bus. We were still a bunch greasy-haired, pimple-faced kids, but there was also an unspoken understanding that this was our first collective step toward a more grandiose stage of maturity—high school.

I was with my good friends, Mike and Steve. We'd been up late the previous night discussing just how much intestinal fortitude it would take to conquer rides like the Demon Drop. It was as if we knew this trip to Cedar Point was more than just a field trip. It was a rite of passage.

Shortly after stepping off the bus, everyone clumped up in their familiar huddles and waited for instructions. Up to this point, our lives had been largely determined by the decisions of our adult supervisors. Honestly, I had never considered myself from any other perspective. Not, that is, until Mike grabbed me by my shirt collar, looked me in the eyes, and said, "Bro, we can do whatever we want. Look around. No one is telling us what to do. Today, this is our park. We have *permission*!"

Mike's words launched all three of us into a new dimension, one in which the world was our oyster. Sure, that world was no bigger than a square mile filled with elephant ears and cotton candy, but to us, it felt like so much more. We were now outside the classroom. Outside the confines that previously defined our reality. I saw my teachers in a different light that day. Suddenly, they looked more like peers than authority figures. We were no longer just kids. That particular day, we were men.

Our newfound freedom gave us a confidence we weren't quite sure what to do with. I don't think any of us could have explained why we reacted the way we did, but with arms locked, we marched through that park saying the same thing over and over, "We. Are on. A mission." It sounds kind of silly now, but it made perfect sense at the time.

Permission produced a mission even when we didn't know what the mission was. It's this "act first, ask questions later" approach that seems to consistently bring God's blessing throughout scripture. Whether it's outside the classroom or outside a church building, there is a fresh mission that awaits those who dare to try something new. For us, on that special day, we found ourselves on an outward trajectory that seemed to change by the hour, but that didn't bother us. We were just glad to be forging our way forward, no longer afraid to ride scary rollercoasters or too intimidated to talk to pretty girls. All we knew was that this was the best day of our lives, and we didn't want it to end.

Maybe you can recall a similar experience, a moment you realized that the world was your oyster. Suddenly, you were free, and a sense of mission began to emerge before you. Perhaps it happened when you got your driver's license or your first car, when you moved out, or went off to college. Maybe it was when you got your first job or married the love of your life. Whenever, and however it started, you felt a sense of adventure and purpose. You were on a mission to make the most of whatever life had for you in that season. *You had permission.*

You probably had no idea how everything would unfold, but like me and my buddies at Cedar Point, fresh permission launched you on an outward trajectory. Unfortunately, most missions like this fizzle because the missions themselves just aren't big enough. Eventually, there are no more roller coasters to ride, driving a car becomes routine, and the new job feels like a chore. Fortunately, that's not the case for all missions.

When you lock arms with God, a mission emerges that is plenty big enough. In addition, it adapts to the unique demands in each season of your life. It's what I'll be referring to as a personal mission—and personal missions never die. They may morph and sometimes stall, but personal missions are resilient. They're a beautiful bond between us and God, that God never lets go of. This is good news! No matter how absent God may seem or how stuck you may feel, your personal mission isn't dead. It's just undeveloped.

Over decades of helping both college students and adults to lock arms with God, I've discovered that there are five distinct stages we need to implement to develop a personal mission beyond the walls of church. The five stages correspond to the five parts of the book. The purpose of this book is to help you navigate all five stages, each one fueled by a common source—permission.

Part 1: Permission to Dream Big. The start of any journey is fun and exciting, but without a big dream as your compass, it won't be long until it feels like you've left the harbor only to be blown off course by the winds of adversity. To counter aimless drift, you need a dream big enough to set your course on a lifelong trajectory. It's here where we'll explore the components of a big dream so you know where your dream is taking you.

Part 2: Permission to Be Armed and Dangerous. Once you are launched in a meaningful and long-lasting direction, both character and intentionality are required to persevere as you explore your personal mission. To remain on the front lines, you will need to resist succumbing to the blandness of conditioned volunteerism. This requires developing holy valor within.

Part 3: Permission to Flip the Script. Anytime we align ourselves with God, we need to understand that his ways are often not our ways. We must look beyond the acceptance of the established order that surrounds us. In order to develop a personal mission that is in step with the life Jesus modeled, you will likely feel out of step with the patterns you have grown accustom to.

Part 4: Permission to Start Fires. In time, your personal mission will likely produce dynamic results you didn't foresee. More and more people will begin to join in, creating a contagious aspiration of kingdom movement. That's when you'll know you're living in the mystery and power of a spiritual fire you could never pull off on your own. Suddenly, it feels as if the kingdom of heaven is near. If you aren't careful, however, you may fall back into the predictability of static institutionalism. It's at this stage where we often lean on old and familiar structures rather than fanning the flames of the new thing God is doing. To keep moving forward, it's important to understand the chemistry behind spiritual fire building.

Part 5: Permission to Prioritize Play. This final stage of developing a personal mission requires your creative initiative. Your final hurdle is overcoming the paralysis of potential failure. To effectively live out the ongoing experiment that is your personal mission, it's essential to adopt an attitude of play.

My prayer is that as you read, you will find yourself more and more captivated by a purpose that can only be accomplished by locking arms with God. There really is no better way to live. Your good, glorious, and adventurous life awaits.

You have permission.

PART 1

PERMISSION TO DREAM BIG: DEVELOPING PURPOSEFUL DIRECTION

Those who dream by night in the dusty recesses of their minds wake in the day to find that it was vanity: but the dreamers of the day are dangerous men, for they may act their dream with open eyes, to make it possible.
—T. E. Lawrence, Seven Pillars of Wisdom

My body was weak, my breath was short, and panic was setting in. Never had I felt so powerless. The waves were growing more turbulent, and I could barely keep my head above the water. Then, *crash!* A huge wave sent me deep under the surface. It took all my strength just to swim back to a place where I could gasp. There was no way I could keep this up. I had already exerted most of my energy trying to swim against what I later learned was a riptide. As my head bobbed above and below the surface, the deafening roar of the waves crashing around me was pierced only by the sound of my wife's screams from shore, begging for someone to please save her husband. It's a situation I wouldn't wish on my worst enemy.

Hope was slipping away quickly. My best guess was that I was now within my last three minutes of life on earth. There wasn't enough time to call for rescue, and there were only a few other people besides my wife on the beach. If it hadn't been for the off chance that one of those people had a boogie board and took the risk to swim out to me, I would never have had the opportunity to pen this book.

It's true what they say—your life does flash before you when you're about to die, but not with all the details. Those come later if you get the chance. The opportunity to reflect on my life after almost losing it has been one of the greatest graces I've ever received. In hindsight, I could now see how God had been leading me throughout my entire life. Even if I didn't know it at the time. And it was this most recent dramatic rescue that now had me humble enough to see that He had a message for me to share. One that I hope is communicated clearly in the following pages.

After the crisis was over, what stood out most to me was how a lack of purposeful direction that day allowed the elements to take control. I almost lost my life because I let my guard down. I allowed idle drift to lead me into dangerous waters. I hadn't intended to entrust my future to the riptide, but that's what happened. And it's been a reminder ever since of how tragic life can turn whenever we allow our circumstances to control our destiny. Granted, most of the surrounding elements or circumstances in our lives are not likely to be as swift as a riptide. In fact, for most of us, the undertow probably happens more subtly and over years or even decades. However, the consequences can be just as tragic.

That's why the starting point for a personal mission is to give yourself permission to dream big. When you dream big, you protect yourself from the indifference of aimless drift because you know where you're going. Your dream will serve as both a catalyst and a compass, keeping you on a trajectory with purposeful direction. And the bigger your dream, the better it works.

PART 1   PERMISSION TO DREAM BIG: DEVELOPING PURPOSEFUL DIRECTION

1. BIG SOURCE

Finding the kind of purposeful direction that becomes a lifelong trajectory is no small task. It won't happen by rolling out of bed and doing whatever strikes your fancy. A long-lasting personal mission can only come from a big dream that captures your soul. Until a dream nestles within your chest and becomes part of you, it will never be more than a big hope or a big idea. A big dream should touch a place so deep within you that it permeates your entire life. It needs to be in your blood. It needs to be in your DNA. And it needs to be anchored to an unshakeable source of power—God himself. When you bring God into redeeming that one thing that breaks your heart, it's a recipe for a life-long mission.

Author and pastor Frederick Buechner captured this beautifully when he wrote, "The place God calls you to is the place where your deep gladness and the world's deep hunger meet." In other words, the sweet spot of purposeful direction is where our deep purpose and God's great power collide. This is the catalyst that launches us into a personal mission with sustainable power.

For over twenty-five years, I had the privilege of living at the intersection of these two power sources in my role as campus minister at Illinois State university. I loved working with students who were old enough to be frustrated with the pain of this fallen world, yet young enough to believe they could do something about it. Throw God into this equation and, *boom!* It was a breeding ground for meaningful and long-lasting personal missions to take root.

What I learned from my time as a campus minister is that God honors intentionality. We don't have to be saints to receive a personal mission. God wants to use all of us. Whether we are men or women, young or old, clean or dirty, His invitation is the same. And all that is required is a posture of surrender. When we intentionally offer ourselves to him in that way, he will instill in us something selfless and fulfilling—a dream. It's what he wants to do. We just have to position ourselves in a way that allows us to hear what God is saying.

There are any number of ways to be intentional about listening to God. You might hear God best when you sit by a lake and reflect on the events of the past month. Maybe you marinate your mind and heart with a daily Bible verse on your commute to work or take a morning walk once a week just to listen. The activity and frequency you choose isn't as important as the intentionality with which you do it. God has a way of noticing our patterns and meeting us within them. I've seen him do it time and time again.

If consistently listening to God is a struggle for you, I encourage you start afresh by scheduling a new time and place to meet—ideally, in a place that takes some effort to get to. Whether it's a lake out in the country or a rooftop view from downtown, God matches our intentionality. Getting away isn't meant to replace the regular times and places you have already established, but to help you connect with God in a new way. Think of it as a kickstart. When we intentionally disrupt our routines by carving out a space for God to meet us, that place immediately holds power—the kind of power that can become a launching pad, catalyzing us into a purposeful direction.

In the Bible, such set-apart ground often played a big role in God's plan to dispatch his people on a personal mission. The burning bush was the launching pad from which God commissioned Moses to free the Israelites. It was a random place on a road that served as the launching pad to commission Paul to preach to the Gentiles. What place might God use to launch you into your personal mission? For me, my staff, and students, that launching pad was an annual pilgrimage to a rustic camp about thirty miles out of town.

Fall Retreat

Every year in late September, I left campus at noon on a Friday and returned on Sunday around the same time. These forty-eight hours away became something I looked forward to all year. God never failed to speak to me, and I was filled with anticipation about what surprise God had waiting for me each year. One year, he invited me to rest. Three years before that, he reminded me that I was forgiven. Some years, the messages repeated, but always with a freshness that was a signature of the Spirit of God. As different as each year was, the retreat always culminated with God sending each of us out with a renewed commitment to our personal mission.

What had started as a spontaneous overnight getaway with a couple carloads of students had grown into something much larger—an event that now included about 200 students, staff, and alumni volunteers. There was nothing particular about the campground, the staff, or the students that made this weekend so significant. The weekend was powerful because of our unwavering belief that God would meet us there. It's an experience I wish everyone could have, and there is one retreat that especially stands out in my memory. I'd like to take you along as I replay that special weekend from years ago.

Arrival

After parking my car, I make my way to the kitchen to check in with the food volunteers. These are my alumni. They serve for the weekend to give students the same gift they received years ago—a distraction-free weekend with Jesus. The kitchen counters are full of bulk food being sorted for the next two days. The conversation is filled with jokes and laughter. I feel like a proud dad who enjoys seeing his kids get along.

Then the conversation seems to steer its way back to the weekend at hand and the nostalgia it evokes in each of them. Everyone seems to have a personal story of life change from this place. It's what draws them back to happily serve as volunteers. No one explicitly states this, but it's clear that each of them is here not just to serve but to tap into that refining power source once again—to be renewed. It's a privilege to be a part of this holy weekend, and the volunteers know it.

Shortly thereafter, students start to show up in a steady stream. The energy is crackling, and the crowd is growing. This opportunity to create new relationships in a new place with the promise of new experiences is a college student's paradise. They all seem to have this beautiful ability to be both serious and fun.

I love seeing their creativity emerge full force as they gather in preassigned groups designated by color. The silliness of rallying around a common color evokes a beautiful combination of lightheartedness and competition. I have it on good word that many of these students have been making runs to the thrift store all week for clothing in their color. Some even come in color-themed costumes. The banana outfit is probably my all-time favorite. The excitement is high, and the bond among us is real.

The colors and competition are the focus as students arrive and settle in together, but everyone who's been here before knows it's not the main event. An encounter with God is coming. An encounter that will not only renew us individually but also transform this community of misfit college students into one body. We know that time will be tomorrow night. And we know the place. That sacred spot where God meets us year after year—the campfire.

Anticipation

You might think that the power of an annual retreat would come through something new: a new format, a new speaker, a new game. But for our retreat, the standard Saturday night campfire is the ultimate destination. It is the place where our great needs come face to face with God's great provision. But I'm getting ahead of myself. For now, we are all busy learning new names and establishing an atmosphere of trust.

Throughout this weekend, I'll be busy tuning my ears to student conversations over meals and late-night discussions. Then I'll spend some time alone with God. I'll ask him what his message is for us, and then I'll listen. After many years of this, I've learned not to have my Saturday night campfire speech polished and ready ahead of time. Why should I? It's going to change anyway. Did I mention that I loved this?

Close to 200 students are now gathered in a gymnasium for our Friday night opening worship time. Anticipation is in the air, with an absolutely electric buzz of energy. Most of the students still have no idea what is coming, but they've heard from others that the fall retreat is the best thing we do. Returning students now expect each year's retreat to top or at least match what they experienced the year before. Am I nervous that they will be disappointed? Not at all. I know what our secret is—a date with our divine power source at the campfire tomorrow night.

I am confident God will show up. I've learned that my job is not to summon the Holy Spirit, but to clear some space, limit distractions, and unite us around a moment in God's presence. I can't put my finger on how God will show up this year, I just have an unwavering trust that he will. Just as he did last year and the years before that. Not knowing how God will show up is part of the excitement. Yet, knowing he will is why we are all here. To be honest, I need this retreat as much or more than the students do.

I breathe a silent prayer. *Lord, please come. Renew my personal vow and clean my cluttered soul. Please speak to me. Give me a message that is relevant for everyone. Thank you for always providing that word. Always.*

I never question that God will answer that prayer. I think it has something to do with intentionally getting close to the source. At the retreat, we are not just talking *about* God, we are talking *with* God. We are seeking his face. We are in pure pursuit mode. It's an honor to be in an environment where God finds a way to bless people who are ready to obey. I want to be one of those people. Again, this isn't just for the students. I know I need to be ready to turn from my own distractions and set my course afresh. This is the kind of work that can only be accomplished by a big power source. Gosh, I love this time.

Fire

It's now Saturday afternoon. We've barely been here for twenty-four hours, and already there are lots of heavy issues coming to the surface. Addictions, sexual abuse, and self-harm, to name a few. It's clear God wants to take those things, to exchange bondage for freedom. I sense he wants this to be more than a night where his kids get a pat on the head, more than mere reassurance that everything will one day be okay. *No.* He wants to destroy spiritual strongholds. He wants to flex his power and annihilate these dark enemies. He wants to reestablish himself as our great power source. We aren't playing youth group games tonight. The seriousness of this moment is ramping up.

Earlier in the week, I bought a wooden chest. It's really nice, classy looking—like something your grandma would have in her attic to store precious memorabilia. We are going to use it to store all of our spiritual junk and then burn it in the campfire. My hope is that it will feel slightly disturbing or even offensive to burn such a nice piece of furniture. I want us all to feel the gravity of what it represents—how we can't always separate the ugly from the beautiful and that all things need to be refined because sin touches every part of our lives. It feels like God is preparing us for a powerful night. The students seem to be acutely aware of the obstacles that keep them from being free, and yet also hopeful that God will provide a way forward.

Things are lining up better than I thought. The Scripture, stories, and conversations are all leading us to a pinnacle moment. Just as we planned. Just as I'd hoped. There is only one problem.

The sky.

It's looking very dark. This is not just a little rain we're talking about but a serious storm. But we can't rush the pre-campfire process. Could we wait until morning? Eh, that would not be the same.

I talk to the staff, and we decide to proceed as planned. I suddenly remember a past retreat when the rain miraculously went around us. That would be a cool story, right? We stop and pray, but the sky is growing darker. We start the fire. Meanwhile, we lead the students through a series of reflective activities. They are encouraged to transfer their struggles, addictions, and sins from that unspoken place within their souls onto pieces of paper, open and exposed.

What started as a spattering of rain is now a torrent as the wind whips the rain against the glass doors. With laser focus, the students appear to have blocked out the weather distractions. All the papers are now tossed into the chest—a combination of pain, sin, and failure fill it to the brim. The students and I are primed to address this chest full of hardships and disappointments. I let them know we will walk down to the campfire where we will burn the chest. They turn their eyes to the storm outside and then back to me. There is a hesitancy in the air, but I assure them that there is a fire blazing in the distance if they are willing to brave the storm. I see the determination in their eyes.

We walk out the door united as a community, pursuing our only hope: Jesus. He's the fire, our great power source. Everyone is eager, but that first step outside brings with it a brisk and wet slap to the face. It's also very dark, and I wonder if most will be tempted to turn back inside where it's safe and dry. To my amazement, the students keep walking. Initially, they are fueled by peer pressure but soon are pulled in by the light of the blazing fire. Sheesh! It's big. And mesmerizing. The rain is falling harder now, yet it appears to have no effect on the intensity of the flames.

Students are huddling together with their hoodies pulled tight, but there is no escaping the penetrating elements. We are all getting soaked, but we are doing it together. There's a shared resilience that keeps us firmly planted. We aren't leaving until our business with God is taken care of.

I begin to preach. The metaphor is so obvious that this message is preaching itself. This fire represents a source of power who is on our side and ready to help us brave the storms we are helpless to navigate on our own. I feel my voice getting louder and louder—partly to compensate for the sound of the wind and rain, but mostly because I am desperate for God to do something he alone can do. With a few more words, I ask that the chest be thrown on the fire.

It feels even more odd than I imagined tossing such a nice piece of furniture into an inferno, but no one questions it. We know what it contains. As the fire swallows up the chest, there is a tangible feeling of release in the air, a feeling that comes only from freedom at the cost of sacrifice. It moves me. I try to keep talking but I'm emotional. The students break into song. Praise is the only proper response. I've got goosebumps on goosebumps. There is something very real and powerful happening in our midst, and I feel so fortunate to be here.

It's been over fifteen years since that retreat, but I will never forget how we stood arm in arm in a rainstorm around an all-consuming fire. It was holy ground. In that moment, we were both freed from the past and catapulted into the future. Personal mission was the natural outcome. It always is. Experiencing Jesus as a recipient is only half of the equation. Taking Him to our unique setting is where purposeful direction starts and where the kingdom really grows. Too often, these catapulting moments are thwarted. Instead of being launched in a purposeful direction, we convince ourselves that these powerful encounters with God are mere stand-alone experiences amid the sea of aimless drift. Sure, these moments fade over time, but we must remember the role they play. It's important to never forget that everything God does is a preparation for something new. He is always preparing and pointing His people to a new thing, a new goal, a new mission, or at least a freshness to our current mission.

You Can Do This

Your launching pad, the set-apart ground that enables you to listen to God, doesn't need to be shared with 200 people. It doesn't need to be elaborately planned or led by paid ministers. When receiving or renewing your personal mission, the only essential is God himself. While he may sneak up and surprise you, it's more likely that he will match your intentionality as you seek his guidance and his power to set you on a lifelong course. A purposeful direction.

What do you need most from God? What are you desperate to find? What breaks your heart? These are the questions that are foundational to finding a personal mission that lasts a lifetime. God's promise is, "You will seek me and find me when you seek me with all your heart" (Jeremiah 29:13 NLT). Therefore, I encourage you to find a place where you can do that—where you can bare your soul and seek God with all your heart. A place where you can be loud. A place where you can be desperate. God loves this sort of thing. Remember, he is willing to meet you more than halfway. It's what he does. So, where could you go to be intentional about meeting with God, your power source?

I don't know what storm might be keeping you from going outside and drawing close to God. I don't know what excuses or doubts may be clouding your perception. But I promise that a new or refreshed personal mission may be just one meeting away. God actually wants you to experience the fulfillment of your dream more than you do. His only requirement is a keen recognition of your need for him and a willingness to boldly approach his white-hot throne.

2. BIG ADVENTURE

Lisa is a stay-at-home mom who is well connected to a growing and diverse network of other moms in her community. She's troubled that many of these women struggle with loneliness, and she dreams about creating a space for connecting these women to each other as well as to God. However, she tells herself that she probably isn't qualified to organize or lead something like this. So, she doubles down on her involvement with the existing programs at her local church, hoping they will fulfill or at least pacify her longing to make a difference. Each night, she prays that her friends will somehow, on their own, cross the hurdles necessary to join her at church on an upcoming Sunday.

CJ is a mechanic whose auto repair shop is surrounded by low-income housing. He has some ideas of how to use his skills to help those in the neighborhood, but he needs some financial help to get started. As he approaches his church for assistance, the conversation turns from helping those in need to building a program that grows the church's Sunday attendance. He feels as if his dream is being hijacked, so he quits.

Sydney is full of fresh ideas about how to transform her surrounding community with Jesus' good news. Although she's only twenty-two, she already has inroads to the entrepreneurial world. She has some pretty innovative ideas, but within her church she is considered too young to implement them. Even if the church leaders would support her, she is hesitant to attach her plans too closely to the ministries of her church. Her peers, who are all too aware of church scandals and failed Christian leaders, would never understand. She feels stuck, alone, unsupported, and is learning to squelch any big dreams that relate to the gospel.

Lisa, CJ, and Sydney all have dreams that tap into their sense of adventure. And yet, the idea of pursuing that adventure appears to have been trained out of them by what they've experienced at church. To be fair, I don't believe this is what most churches intend. I have several minister friends who all deeply want to empower their members. Nonetheless, Lisa, CJ, and Sydney would all confess that taking a risk to pursue their God-given dreams has been replaced with feelings of resignation and weariness. As a result, they've lost that one thing the apostle Paul warns us never to lose—our calling.

In his letter to the church at Ephesus, Paul writes, "Live a life worthy of the calling you have received" (Ephesians 4:1). Calling is an interesting word, one that many of us, including me, have grown scared of. It sounds so certain, so specific, as if there is just one role or one task God has for us—and if we're not careful, we might miss it. However, a closer look at the kind of calling Paul is talking about reveals that calling is less about a role or task than it is a passion for a particular way of life. Paul doesn't seem concerned about the specifics of how we live out our calling, but that we live a life worthy of our calling. In other words, that we don't settle for a life without divine adventure.

When Lisa, CJ, and Sydney set aside their adventurous ideas, they were doing more than just postponing an opportunity; they were actually setting aside their passions, and then the hope and excitement of what could be slowly faded until they became bored and indifferent. This is what Paul was warning us against. Don't settle! Instead, live a life worthy of the calling you have received.

So, what about you? When was the last time you felt that sense of divine adventure, an invitation to take a risk to make a difference in the world? How did you respond? Do you feel like you've had to squelch your passion for a particular way of life? To settle for a less worthy life?

The divine adventure God calls us to isn't a bonus or a perk. It's foundational. The Greek word for church is *ecclesia*. Literally translated, it means a gathering of the "outward called," or a gathering of those who are passionate about a particular way of life. In other words, every person in a church is expected to be on an adventurous personal mission that takes them out into the world. Sadly, this is hardly the current reality in most churches. And yet, finding and sustaining a sense of adventure must be at the core of our personal mission or it will fade like everything else.

My Big Adventure

Although I'd grown up in church, it wasn't until the end of my sophomore year in college that I first understood the gospel as it was intended—as good news. This, as it turns out, was more than a ticket to heaven. It was God's willingness to make up the difference in all aspects of my life, even those things that weren't so spiritual. When I began to see that God was on my side, something flipped. It was then that I became an ambassador for this gospel. I figured if I was privy to the best news available, why wouldn't I leverage my whole life to both live it and share it? Immediately, I began to see how the gospel had a way of blessing the messenger as much or more than the recipients of that message. It was an exciting and liberating time. No longer was my faith limited to a creed I mechanically recited once a week in church. I was now filled with a sense of purpose. A calling was developing. Adventure was brewing because I wanted to make the most of my one and only life.

The way I saw it, God was big, and if the two of us were friends, we could do big things together. Maybe even change the world. For the first time ever, I began to see myself as a free agent for God, available to be dispatched to any sector he saw fit. This new perspective brought with it a surprise gift I hadn't seen coming—a big dream. It was that mere announcement I heard the week before about an upcoming mission trip that was now, in this very moment, transforming into something epic. I was suddenly consumed with an opportunity and adventure I had previously never considered. There is something powerful about being so right with God, that moments like this sneak up on you, even while driving on the backroads in rural Michigan. Moments when all your insecurities fade away, and God stands before you saying, "let's do this thing." The details were still fuzzy of course, but I knew in this moment that God was picking me to do something. I felt like God was my teammate and coach rolled into one, and we were at the start of a historic playoff run. I had to pull the car over to let the gravity of this moment settle in. I was about to embark on the first of many acts God had prepared for me. An act that would include six other young people on a year-long mission to the country of Hungary.

As I sat in that front seat of my '78 Malibu, I was overrun with one thought. How did I get here? How did this dream just download to my soul? I was under the assumption that God only delivered these sorts of life-altering invitations to people in dramatic ways who were going through some tragic crisis. But that wasn't my case. My life was pretty ordinary and unassuming at the time. I was still living at home. My friends and relatives were healthy. I was passing all my classes, and my girlfriend hadn't broken up with me. At least, not yet. In addition, this moment was not marked with the dramatic flair I would have expected either. I wasn't at a Christian concert or camp. There was no persuasive speaker or dynamic band. Heck, there wasn't even another human being within a square mile of me. I experienced literally none of the events I assumed were associated with receiving a big dream. So again, how did I get here? This, as it turns out, was my first experience with what we discussed in the previous chapter. An intentionality with God that produced a launching pad. In this case, right here in the front seat of my '78 Malibu.

My drive home was one that I will never forget. The windows were down, and the breeze brought with it a fresh scent of adventure. My mind was racing, my heart was full, and I felt excitement brewing within me. The *Shawshank Redemption* wouldn't be released for a few more years, but I was already experiencing what would soon be Morgan Freeman's epic line from that movie: "I think it's the excitement only a free man can feel, a free man at the start of a long journey whose conclusion is uncertain."

I was indeed a free man, and my freedom was multifaceted. Sure, I was just a twenty-year-old kid, so it wasn't like I had a lot of burdens or responsibilities. I had no debt. No mortgage. No family obligations, and certainly, no career pressures. Yup, I was free. But never had I felt a freedom like this. I was on the cusp of something beautifully unknown, and full of adventure.

Strange as it might sound, it was at this profound moment, right there in the front seat of my car, when I was revisited by my invisible friend from childhood. It had been fifteen years or more since I last experienced this comforting illusion. I know, invisible friends are weird—don't judge. You'll have to trust me that this is just what kids did in the seventies before there were iPads and cell phones.

Throughout the earliest years of my childhood, whatever new place I visited, whatever new activity I tried, every book I opened, every trip I took, my invisible friend was there with me. There was only one place my friend never accompanied me—church. At church, predictability was king, and adventure was nowhere to be found.

What I realize now is that my invisible friend is a manifestation of something I had no words for as a kid—*anticipation*. So why after all these years was my friend anticipation now back by my side? And why would he show up here, hand in hand with Jesus? I'd never seen these two together before. This was a uniquely powerful moment, where for the first time in my life, I didn't feel the need to choose between adventure and Jesus. My personal mission was taking shape, and I had high hopes that this mission, unlike others, would last—hopefully for a lifetime.

Sustaining Adventure

It's now been thirty-four years since that crisp October afternoon. I'm happy to report that the thrill of anticipation has indeed lasted, and I still feel like I'm on an adventure with God. An adventure that takes what's given to me. With each season comes new opportunities. The same is true for you. Like Lisa, there will be times you find yourself steeped in an abundance of relational richness. Like CJ, your special talents and opportunities will match the surrounding needs, and like Sydney, throughout your life, there will be a plethora of good ideas that run through that brain of yours. Adventure is always lurking just under the surface, but I understand it doesn't come cheap. I want to take a moment to recognize the unique obstacles and challenges you may be facing. I'm aware that you may be confronting things that I will never have to consider. But, like you, I've had my own array of difficulties and setbacks. As a missionary in an underdeveloped country, I took a bath out of a bucket for an entire year, I've felt loneliness over the holidays, and I've felt the pain of losing a firstborn baby due to primitive hospital conditions. But I'm not alone. You too have stories of disappointment and pain. It's unavoidable. I can't speak to your specific situation, but I am sympathetic. I get that it's hard to sustain a sense of adventure when you're going through a tough season. When your stomach is tied in knots from relational conflict. When your thoughts are consumed with financial stresses. And when you feel trapped in a cycle of depression that makes even getting out of bed a real challenge. But hear me when I say, it's amid these obstacles that a mission with God shines the brightest. It's only outside of our comfort zone where a true dependence on God is possible, and where a life of adventure flourishes. It's my belief that our lack of adventure isn't as much a symptom of us being too busy, it's that we are too comfortable. Comfort is predictable. And predictability sends our friend anticipation packing. Consequently, adventure is soon replaced with boredom. A boredom that blurs our ability to even recognize a life worthy of the calling we have received.

But don't let this get you down. The solution is quite simple—permission to embrace the "new." Whether it's new relationships, new environments, or new experiences, God has a way of using new things to keep the spark in your personal mission. What if you made it a goal to explore one new city each spring? To learn one new skill or hobby? Playing an instrument, cycling, or rock climbing could open incredible opportunities that you have no way of seeing now. Chances are that any fresh adventure will dovetail with new friendships. My wife likes to remind me that for every hobby, there is a subculture that surrounds it. Even without a new hobby, imagine what could transpire if you made a weekly goal to meet three new people? Learning simple things about them, like what they do, where they live, and what they enjoy doing, could open incredible doors. At the very least, you'd be on a first name basis with the gas station attendant, the cashier at Menards, and the mail carrier.

The point is that comfort zones kill adventure. And if we want a personal mission that that keeps adventure alive, we must relish new opportunities. Developing a discipline of being open to the new has been a challenge at times, but I can confidently say that it's been worth it. My commitment to following God's lead into new experiences has kept my friend anticipation right there by my side, accompanying me on this grand adventure—and not just to be a missionary in Hungary. That, it turns out, was only the first stop.

3. BIG SCOPE

I had never considered myself a hiker, a camper, or anything of the sort, which is probably why scaling a mountain in the middle of the night struck me as a bad idea. Yet, here I was, slowly working my way up the second highest peak in the Philippines. I was a long way from home and a long way from that original dream God had first planted in me ten years prior as I sat in the front seat of my Chevy Malibu. Cold was setting in and my breath was short. Had it been up to me, I would have turned around an hour earlier, but it wasn't up to me. Plus, I was stuck on a narrow path in the middle of a long, single file line made up of my Filipino friends—a mix of current and former students from a local Philippines-based campus ministry. There were about fifteen of us in total, and there were only two dim flashlights ahead of us to lead the way.

Ben and Chad were the only other Americans joining me on this trek. While the three of us cautiously forged ahead and tried not to be consumed with dangerous "what-if" scenarios, our Filipino friends were laughing and carefree. I don't know how to convey to you just how dark it was toward the back of that long line, but it didn't affect our Filipino friends in the slightest. They never once considered that it might be safer to wait until dawn for the hike. No, they all insisted that we needed to see the sunrise from the summit. And even when we approached some very narrow and dangerous sectors, their cautions for safety were laced with humor. One person would call out in a loud voice, "Heaven, one step to the left!" Then they would all cackle in unison like a gang of merry turkeys. I loved these guys. They were full of passion and fun, and it was their pure joy in the Lord that was now luring me back to work with them in a more official capacity.

It was just a few years before that my wife and I had started this campus ministry in the Philippines. What had begun as a dream to serve for a year in Hungary soon grew into a bigger dream that included more people. That's the way God-dreams work—they grow in scope. The year Paulette and I started the ministry had been full of difficulty and heartache. As I previously mentioned, we lost our first child during that time, but still, there was also undeniable fruit from our work. Years had now passed, Paulette and I had returned to work in the United States, and my relationship to this special ministry had taken the form of long-distance support. Instead of calling the shots, I was more like a supportive big brother. But all of that was about to change on this trip. The scope of my dream was about to broaden once again.

Ben, Chad, and I were here to propose a more official partnership. We saw lots of potential for the ministry to spread throughout the Philippines and, in turn, to eventually send adventure-filled graduates into multiple surrounding countries. We felt that the ministry's need for resources and support was something we could best provide by entering a formal partnership. So, the purpose for this trip was no small task. If we were going to align our ministries into one organization, it would require an agreed-upon vision with a bigger scope.

With a few years of ministry experience under my belt, I was not so naive to think that old friendships alone would be an adequate foundation for an organizational partnership. Plus, I knew we'd have to navigate some cultural and organizational differences, a challenge we would have faced even if the ministry merger had been with another organization in the States. And while I can't recall exactly whose idea it was, we somehow ended up deciding that we could begin to navigate this conversation about a common ministry vision while walking up a mountain together in the pitch dark.

Arnold, the Filipino leader of this ministry, was a dear and close friend. We made it a point to position ourselves together in the single file line so we could talk as we walked. As the morning light slowly lit up the path and our lush surroundings, we both experienced a felt sense of God's presence. It was a beautiful time that I will never forget. God was bringing Arnold's big dream and my big dream together.

As we were about to form a partnership, God deepened and widened our dreams. They were deepened because we were forced to lean even harder into God's leadership, and they were widened because we were casting a bigger net together with the goal of bringing in more and more people. That's part of what it means to have a big scope—that you allow your big dream to lead you into relationships and even partnerships with others who are also pursuing big dreams. I've learned over the years that if your big dream doesn't allow you to play well with others, then it may be that your dream is too small.

As Arnold and I climbed together in the dark, there was no way I could have fathomed that I might one day be called to something even bigger. But it would happen. Fifteen years later, I would stand before my staff, Arnold, and 500 faithful supporters announcing that I was moving on to a new ministry. My message that night will be entitled, "You Can Never Outdream God."

Even in this moment, as I type this chapter, God is continuing to grow my dream by graciously allowing me to bump into humble and righteous people with big dreams of their own from all over the world. Whether they are from China, Spain, Germany, or Chile, these recipients of God's calling are all unified in something deeper and wider than their own agenda. They are unified in a bigger dream.

You'll know you're beginning to experience a big scope when what starts as a unique dream for your own life begins to mature over time and align with the God-dreams of others around you. It's a process that continues until we all share the same grand vision. Again, that's how God-dreams work. There is an inexplicable bond that is formed when you share your dream and another person excitedly proclaims, "God has given me the same dream!"

A Shared Deep Belief

There is an unequivocal rush you experience when you find someone with a big dream that mirrors your own. It's a phenomenon masterfully described by author Simon Sinek in his book *Start with Why*. He states that people are not moved by *what* they do but rather *why* they do it. The *why* is the heart behind a big dream. It's the common denominator everyone can agree on. It's what Sinek refers to as a "shared deep belief,"[1] and it is an essential building block for all movements. It's possible that *what* two people do can be completely different, but if their *why* is the same, it produces a bond that unites them in a shared vision.

Many companies and organizations capitalize on this principle of a shared deep belief. Harley Davidson is one of them. While other motorcycle companies are busy describing their newest model, Harley Davidson is busy promoting adventure and freedom. Their focus is on the *why* rather than the *what*. One of the foundational components to their success is a magazine they've published since 1916 called the *Enthusiast* that features stories of dangerous exploits and cross-country road trips. The Harley Davidson brand has become so synonymous with freedom and adventure that people routinely get tattoos of their logo—something I've never seen people do with Honda, Suzuki, or any other motorcycle brand.

Of course, Jesus understood the power of a shared deep belief. Instead of talking about *what* to believe. He addressed *why* we should believe. While the religious leaders focused on rules and creeds, Jesus passionately offered what every person longed for in their core—freedom, purpose, and belonging. Instead of charts and graphs describing how his ministry would work, he offered membership in a kingdom. This is more than a metaphor and more than a place with borders. God's kingdom is a

---

[1] Simon Sinek, *Start with Why: How Great Leaders Inspire Everyone to Take Action* (New York: Penguin Books, 2009), 147.

domain stretching to wherever the reign of his kingship is recognized. A domain that is ever growing.

The point is, if Jesus came to unleash a kingdom with an unlimited scope, it would also need to scratch the deep itch of all human beings. It would need to be a kingdom as relevant to my college peers as it is to my grandmother and her knitting club. It would need to be inclusive of all cultures and languages all around the world. Indeed, it would need to address the shared deep belief of all people. And here's what we need to understand about the principle hidden within this approach when it comes to our own dreams—the deeper the shared belief, the wider the scope of influence.

That doesn't mean your dream has to be as deep and as wide as the unlimited scope of God's kingdom—at least not initially. However, it does mean your dream should continue to grow in scope over time. Whether you are just starting your journey or have been developing your personal mission for many years, there should always be room for expansion. If your dream isn't growing, it isn't fully alive.

Here is a humbling truth that we are all prone to avoid—You aren't the only one to whom God has given a dream. The sooner we embrace this idea, the better. Because the scope of your God-given dream will only grow in proportion to its ability to align with other dreams. This is why it is essential to listen intently to others. Listen for the passion. Listen for the why. Then allow yourself, even for a moment, to enter their dream and to try it on for size, and see if it fits. If it's too small, kindly return it. But if it's bigger, consider how your dream can grow into theirs. Here are two good litmus test questions to help you assess whether your dream is growing in scope.

Is your dream moving in or moving out? Dreams that move in tend to be limited, but dreams that move out are expansive. For example, CJ wasn't interested in using his dream of a car repair ministry just to fill seats for his church. He wanted to provide a gift that would keep on giving. His dream was moving out because he wanted to bless people so they too could be a blessing. And one day, he might partner with other dreamers to develop a statewide movement of car repair ministries, all stemming from his first humble location. That means that CJ's dream might also get a little messy as it expands because he won't be able to control everything. If you are committed to an ever-broadening scope, you will need to be comfortable with outcomes that are less controlled, managed, or predictable.

Does your dream need to be under a banner with your name on it? There's nothing inherently wrong with uniting under the banner of your name or your organization's name. In fact, it's often necessary. But are you just as willing to unite under someone else's banner to achieve something even bigger? Too many times, I've seen people set aside God's best because of a prideful loyalty to a name on a banner. Sometimes, the name on our banner grows with the size of the dream, but sometimes, our dreams need to be enveloped into something greater—maybe even something that doesn't have anyone's name attached to it accept God's.

Perspective

As we reached the summit, the clouds slowly dissipated into the sun's warm glow, and we could see for miles. Everyone and everything was now at our feet. It's a humbling thing to see the world from God's point of view—and it was from this higher vantage point that I could now see the bigger picture that God had been painting all along. I was able to recognize how my surrender to the biggest source allowed me to experience a big adventure and had now brought me to this perspective of a bigger scope. I felt overcome by gratitude as I stood on that mountain. For whatever reason, God chose to give me a personal mission on a dirt road in Michigan that had now grown into something that enveloped multiple communities on the other side of the world. And it was clear that the scope of this dream would never stop expanding until it benefited all the people in the valley.

PART 2

PERMISSION TO BE ARMED AND DANGEROUS: DEVELOPING HOLY VALOR

No life lacks grandeur if you claim it as your own.
—Marty Rubin

If aimlessness drift is the obstacle to overcome in stage one, then the blandness of conditioned volunteerism is the obstacle to overcome in stage two. Serving as a volunteer has its place, but developing a personal mission beyond the walls of the church requires much more from you than the predictability of working at an event registration table or directing cars in the parking lot. It requires a willingness to become God's agent in the world—and that requires developing holy valor.

To have holy valor is to live with divine courage. It's holy in that you know you have been set apart by God. It's valorous or brave because no personal mission, and I mean *not one*, goes exactly as planned. To pursue your personal mission, you'll need the guts and flexibility to adjust, pivot, or start again whenever things don't go as planned. This is about more than just perseverance or trying harder. It's about developing your God-given character and spiritual gifts so you can draw on them when things get tough. If you want to be armed and dangerous for God—to have a personal mission that sustains you for the long haul—don't skip this stage of the process. Your holy valor will only be as strong as the character and gifts you develop.

PART 2   PERMISSION TO BE ARMED AND DANGEROUS: DEVELOPING HOLY VALOR

4. FULLY ARMED

Early on a rainy morning in September 2012, Derrick prepared himself for another day of work in one of the toughest occupations in America—high school teacher. Preparing lessons was important and essential, but it was only part of what made him so good at his job. Derrick was also committed to preparing himself emotionally and spiritually for his work each day. His job was teaching, but his personal mission was investing in his students. So, he was intentional about building relationships, especially with the loners, even if they failed to reciprocate. And it was hard work. Which is why Derrick armed himself with more than just teaching skills and lesson planning, the skills required for his occupation.

To be the kind of teacher students could trust, Derrick's personal mission required him to also be armed with patience, kindness, integrity, and spiritual maturity. As he walked into my daughter's high school that day, Derrick had no idea just how important this preparation would be.

With just a few minutes left in the first-hour period, one of his students stepped to the front of the class. Derrick knew this young man—one of the loners who was often bullied by other students. It was obvious he was disturbed, and Derrick immediately knew something was wrong. When the student pulled a gun from his duffle bag, a series of terrifying events followed. The student issued threats and fired shots, but Derrick was ultimately able to subdue him before anyone was injured.

It was an ordinary teacher with a fully armed character who saved lives when things didn't go as planned that day. And it's the fully armed character within you that will enable you to face the challenges of pursuing your own personal mission.

So, what does it look like to have a fully armed character and how do we know if we have one? Perhaps the best starting point is to consider what the apostle Paul describes as a life characterized by either good fruit or bad fruit.

Good and Bad Fruit

In his letter to the church at Galatia, Paul encourages believers to live fully armed by the power of the Holy Spirit. That's when our lives are characterized by good fruit. He writes, "But the Holy Spirit produces this kind of fruit in our lives: love, joy, peace, patience, kindness, goodness, faithfulness, gentleness, and self-control" (Galatians 5:22–23 niv).

Note that Paul says it is the Holy Spirit who produces this fruit in us. In other words, we don't produce good fruit in our lives by working hard at trying to be joyful, patient, kind, and all the rest. Instead, these are all byproducts of investing in an intimate relationship with God. And isn't it consistent with God's nature to produce fruit in our lives not from striving and trying harder but from drawing close to him and resting in him? It's this posture of surrender and trust that enables the Holy Spirit to be at home within us. Although drawing close to God requires intentionality on our part, we can rely on the work of the Holy Spirit to produce fruit in our lives that is both beautiful and astounding.

Conversely, when we hold tightly and anxiously to the reigns of life, determined to live on our own terms, another list of fruit emerges that is not so beautiful. Paul details this list of bad fruit as well:

> When you follow the desires of your sinful nature, the results are very clear: sexual immorality, impurity, lustful pleasures, idolatry, sorcery, hostility, quarreling, jealousy, outbursts of anger, selfish ambition, dissension, division, envy, drunkenness, wild parties, and other sins like these. (Galatians 5:19–21 niv)

If we want to be fully armed with strong character, these two lists provide clear pictures of what that does and does not look like in everyday life. The lists also serve as a framework we can use to assess where we are right now and to identify where we want to be. We need that because without a clear standard to measure ourselves against, we'll likely settle for who we are rather than who we could become.

To be honest, there have been seasons in my life when I deceived myself into thinking my character was healthier than it was. I suppose we all tend to believe we are basically good people and that we are living at least close to the best version of ourselves. However, when it comes to character, the litmus test is to consider the words and actions of our past four to six months and ask the uncomfortable yet revealing question, "Which list are my words and actions characterized by—good fruit or bad fruit?"

To live armed by the power of the Spirit requires routinely taking an unflinching look in the mirror of your life—not to run yourself down but to identify opportunities for growth. If you are going to have the character it takes to lead a life with an effective personal mission, this is an essential discipline to master. It's also one of the hardest disciplines to practice because, again, we tend to deceive ourselves into thinking we're healthier than we are. It's a dynamic I routinely witnessed in my work as a campus minister. And often, it was those who considered themselves the strongest Christians who ended up being the most deceived, which made them dangerous in our community. It was almost as if they were devoted to arming themselves with bad fruit (what Paul characterized as "rivalries, dissensions, and divisions") rather than arming themselves with the fruit of good character. While this sort of character deficiency isn't always as pronounced as it is in the story I'm about to share, the consequences are always felt.

I once had a situation in which a Christian group who were preoccupied with dramatic manifestations of the Holy Spirit[2] saw our campus community as a perfect recruiting ground for their ministry. They bypassed any interaction with me as the leader and never even considered visiting our large group meeting. Instead, they approached a handful of my students directly and invited themselves over to introduce them to what they promised was a better and fuller experience of God. When they arrived, they cleared the room of furniture and proceeded to loudly and emphatically create a chaotic scene that included speaking in tongues, slaying one another in the Spirit, and barking like dogs!

Their actions created a real mess, sowing seeds of distrust, anger, and confusion throughout our ministry. In fact, it was so divisive I was forced to hold an emergency meeting. Up to that point, I'd never felt the need to have such a meeting. There was great tension as members of this group were present, and it was clear they were ready for a debate. Their supporting text was, "Do not get drunk on wine, which leads to debauchery. Instead, be filled with the Spirit" (Ephesians 5:18 niv). They claimed this verse was textual proof of the need for Christians to get "drunk" on the Spirit.

I was glad to have a friend and counterpart present to help me sort through this mess of immaturity. He began by asking what the opposite of being drunk with wine would look like. He then read aloud the two lists from Galatians 5, which of course concluded with the fruit of self-control. This clear and concise explanation was exactly what we needed. In a very confusing and tension-filled moment, God's Word brought peace and clarity. The practical conclusion was obvious to all—self-control is the exact

---

[2] I want to be clear that I respect the beliefs and practices of the charismatic community. I have been blessed to be present on many occasions when the Holy Spirit was evident in what some might consider nonconventional ways. The point I want to make in telling this story is that the members of this particular group were not armed with the fruit of the Spirit. Instead, they were preoccupied with the gifts of the Spirit, which made them dangerous disruptors in our midst.

opposite of losing control or of "drunkenness" in any form. After making this point, the debate ended, but I've never forgotten it.

Weeks later, a student let me know that this confusing and emotional situation was clarified for her by observing the stark contrast of fruit in the lives of those on either side of the debate. It was clear to her that there was a distinct presence of peace, patience, and kindness from our side of the room. Without even understanding the specifics of the theological debate, it was our character she trusted. Ever since, I've made a point to assess the trustworthiness of others based on the visible fruit in their lives, and the apostle Paul's two-list filter has helped me to clear up many complicated situations. I've also come to understand that people can fool you through fast-talking arguments, but the fruit of their lives never lies.

Perhaps you've had similar experiences in which you had an uneasy sense that something was off; a time when a person's words and actions didn't seem to match. If you want to have an effective personal mission, you need to do the work to make sure you are never that person. And one of the best ways to guard against the danger of self-deception in assessing your character is to invite input from others.

Invite Input from Others

It's always much easier to detect poor character in others than it is to detect it in ourselves. No matter how well intentioned you are when you look at your character in the mirror, it will be challenging to assess yourself objectively. Most of us need help to see ourselves clearly, which is why it's essential to invite a couple of trustworthy friends to speak candidly about what they see when they look at the fruit of our life.

During my time as a campus minister, we took this standard of a fruit-filled character so seriously that when selecting student leaders, we created a process that included multiple sources of input. We believed Jesus' statement that, "Every good tree bears good fruit, but a bad tree bears bad fruit. A good tree cannot bear bad fruit, and a bad tree cannot bear good fruit" (Matthew 7:18 niv).

We understood that the best way to detect a good tree was to wait and see what fruit fell from that tree. But we also soon learned that it wasn't fair to evaluate people through only one or two lenses. We needed multiple perspectives. A common phrase we adopted was to "look for fruit in people's rearview mirror." In other words, we looked back at the previous six months to see what fruits of the Spirit were evident in that person's life and relationships. If our potential student leader talked a good talk but was on his fourth girlfriend in two months, we knew we had a problem. And we used the same standard in assessing relationships with the student's boss, roommates, and even parents. We weren't looking for perfection but simply observing which list from Galatians 5 most recently characterized their life.

It was always interesting to see who made the cut for our student leadership team. Some of the extroverted people I might have expected to make the list often didn't, and some of the quiet people ended up being some of our best leaders. We quickly learned that what God looks for in a leader often differs from what the world looks for in a leader. Appreciation for these fruit-filled people was a constant source of inspiration to our staff. And it was this culture of good fruit that inspired us as to live our own lives in the same fruit filled manner. We were all in this together.

The Power of Good Fruit

It became clear to us that even when our fruit-filled students were unclear of their personal mission, they still had a way of being surprisingly effective at expanding God's kingdom. I think we often underestimate how compelling good fruit is and how magnetic it can be. There is no denying that people with good fruit are more respected, listened to, and flat out more attractive.

That meant our good fruit student leaders made a positive impact on others simply by being in proximity to them. They didn't always have to spend a lot of time figuring out where they were going or what their mission was because God's mission found them. Whether it was through their role as roommates, classmates, or teammates, God routinely blessed our well-armed students with opportunities to be good news in ways that helped others to experience life transformation.

Let this be an encouragement to you. If you are still confused or even frustrated about what your personal mission might be, don't stress. Regardless of how clear or unclear you may be about the specific mission God may be calling you to, your life will always have impact when you're focused on developing your character and producing good fruit. Remember, God isn't looking for people with big ideas of their own. Rather, he is looking for people who have the strength of character to carry out his big ideas. The less you obsess about the big thing you are supposed to do, the better the chances you will find yourself positioned for whatever and whoever God brings your way.

Once you're armed with good character, a whole new world of opportunity will open itself to you. One that leverages your fruit-filled life toward action. Being fruit-filled isn't the whole story. We are also created to be dangerous. Unfortunately, to be armed but not dangerous—in the sense of dangerous for God—is an all-too-common scenario. In the next chapter, we'll take a closer look at what it looks like to unleash our dangerously bright gifts.

5. DANGEROUSLY BRIGHT

As Christians, we live out holy valor when we choose to be light bearers. Light is the one thing that Satan fears. Afterall, darkness is the environment in which Satan does his most devious work. It's in the darkness where sin remains a secret, where brokenness goes unacknowledged, and where truth becomes lies. There is nothing more dangerous to the kingdom of darkness than the light of Jesus.

In his earthly ministry, Jesus' most powerful weapon was illumination. Sure, he could perform miracles, but it was his ability to shine light on forgotten people, abandoned places, and hardened hearts that was his forte. Light was Jesus' primary weapon. And this was not a weapon he "carried" so much as someone he "became." In a way, Jesus was a transformer. He took on the form of light that was most needed in any given situation.

If we are to be like Jesus as we live out our purpose in the world, we too need to become dangerously bright. We do that by identifying and developing our God-given spiritual gifts. In his letter to the church at Ephesus, the apostle Paul identifies five gifts, each one a unique form of light we can wield in the world.

> So Christ himself gave the apostles, the prophets, the
> evangelists, the pastors (shepherds) and teachers, to
> equip his people for works of service, so that the body of
> Christ may be built up until we all reach unity in the faith
> and in the knowledge of the Son of God and become
> mature, attaining to the whole measure of the fullness of
> Christ. (Ephesians 4:11–13 NIV)

Although God has wired each of us to have natural tendencies toward probably one or two spiritual gifts, I believe we also have the ability and responsibility to wield multiple forms of light—to "transform" as Jesus did—depending on what the situation requires. These gifts are who we become as we take on the likeness of Jesus. With time and practice, we can develop not only our primary gifts but also develop the ones that are not as natural. Understanding how you are naturally gifted with light and how to leverage that light is key to unleashing God's most dangerously effective tool—you. In this chapter, we will explore each of the five gifts to help you discern which one(s) God has given you. Like Jesus, God's dangerously bright light is also in you. And there are five distinct places we can shine that light. We can shine it on the word of God, the people around us, the good news, the heart of God, or the path ahead.

Apostle: Illuminator of the path ahead

Those with the gift of apostleship are spiritual entrepreneurs. The biblical description literally means to be a "sent one," or to be a missionary. Apostles are driven by a desire to expand the kingdom of heaven. Where others see dead ends, these people see opportunity. Apostles use their light to help others see what's possible, and they have a knack for casting a vision of what could and should be. It's the apostles who light the way into new territories—they help us see a school, a youth center, or a business before they exist. They also have an uncanny ability to get these efforts off the ground.

Chad is an example of a gifted apostle. Chad was a townie, meaning he lived in a university town, but, unlike his friends from high school, he wasn't accepted to the university when he applied. He felt angry, lonely, and lost and wasn't sure what to pursue next. Eventually, he made his way into our campus ministry through the invitation of a friend. Chad and I hit it off, and he soon became a leader in our group. But Chad's leadership looked a little different and rough around the edges, which was initially a challenge for me.

Chad didn't want to regurgitate Bible studies or have standard discipleship meetings. He'd say things that were unrefined or joke about things that were a bit off color. He listened to rap music and referred to himself as "Chaddy MacDaddy." He wanted to do things on his own and in his own way. In most Christian circles, a guy like Chad would probably have been seen as unpredictable and certainly not fit for leadership. I'll admit, I had been burned by unteachable students before, so I was cautious, but over time, Chad proved that his independent streak wasn't rooted in rebellion. He just wanted to create things that didn't currently exist. He wanted to shed light on something new.

Chad started more initiatives in our ministry than any other student during my tenure. He was always generating new ideas, new games, and new events. One year, he convinced about twenty people to join him for a ridiculous idea that grew into a tradition, bonding our students around a disgusting event called Meat Week. The idea was for all participants to eat nothing but meat for seven full days. It was a hit, even though it left everyone constipated and our small ministry house smelling like Canadian bacon for weeks afterward. But before you start to think of Chad as nothing more than a crazy kid gone rogue, you need to hear the rest of his story.

I took Chad on his first mission trip to the Philippines. It was here that I really started to see how Chad always shed light on things that didn't yet exist. He was already in the process of starting his own business, and it didn't surprise me one bit that he made connections with our Filipino friends, inviting them to work for his start-up company. He developed a partnership and a team that still works with him more than seventeen years later.

Upon his trip home, instead of reminiscing about that particular trip, he decided to organize his own trip to Kenya to visit a ministry that served those living in a neglected slum. When the ministry he visited turned out to be disorganized and ineffective, he began to wander the streets of the slum on his own. He quickly observed that much of the suffering he witnessed could be addressed with simple medicines and basic education. It was this vision of what could and should be that poured out of him when we had a follow-up breakfast a week after his return. Through tears, he said, "Pete, I told myself that I just can't ignore this. I had to do something. There are too many people doing nothing! I can't do that. So, I'm starting my own organization, and I'm calling it GOYA Ministries. GOYA stands for 'Get Off Your Ass.'"

Chad did indeed start the organization. GOYA Ministries' work is now multifaceted, not only providing medicine, food, and clean water but also starting multiple churches and establishing one of the most respected high schools in the Nairobi area. Today, Chad is an elder at a large church and a successful entrepreneur and has matured to a significant place of leadership within his community. He is both armed and dangerously bright for the kingdom.

There is no doubt that spiritual entrepreneurs, especially young ones, can walk the fine line of being dangerously effective or flat out dangerous. I want to encourage you to curb your temptation to avoid such people. Remember, those with the gift of apostleship have little to lose. The church, on the other hand, has a lot to lose if we sideline guys like Chad. Both Chad and I would agree that his maturity came when someone gave him a real seat at the table—a seat that allowed him to accomplish his greatest passion, which is expansion. There is nothing an apostle wants more than to take new ground for the kingdom.

Do you resonate with Chad's story? Do you stay up at night dreaming of new possibilities? Do you feel like the only thing that stands in the way of your revolutionary new business, nonprofit, or ministry is a few people to help you execute? Do you feel like the more you try to shed light on new opportunities, the more you are written off as a person who is unfocused or unrefined?

If you find yourself in this frustrating cycle, remember that your role as an illuminator of new territory is critical. God has gifted you to see what others can't. He gifted you with apostleship for a reason and wants you to keep shining your light on the path ahead, to envision and create what doesn't yet exist.

If God has called you to be an apostle, receive this commissioning.

You are a dream awakener. A catalyst for more. You are God's sent one. You are meant to cross boundaries, to be a pioneer. You are meant to cultivate a community of discipleship where everything multiplies. You constantly envision new ways for disciples, ministries, churches, and movements to grow. What others see as a dead end, you see as a unique opportunity. God has made you a visionary for expansion, a light shining on new possibilities. Now, go be you.

Prophet: Illuminator of the heart of God

People with the gift of prophecy expose what is under the surface. Biblically, prophets are messengers of God. They have a way of helping people become aware of their true motives while simultaneously revealing the heart of God. Prophets are fueled by the Holy Spirit and are passionate about cultivating environments that foster intimacy with God. These people can be both those eccentric types who squint their eyes as they gently provide divine insight and those justice types who boldly stand with the oppressed. They have no problem being both the person who points upward to God and the one who drops that same finger into the chest of the one who is hurting God's heart. Prophets are uniquely able to see what God sees, feel what God feels, and use those insights to advance God's kingdom.

There is no one who has illuminated the heart of God in my life more than a student named Leah. When Leah first came into our ministry, she was a loner, and I didn't understand her. Her attire was simple, and she appeared to be somewhat aloof. She didn't talk about the same things others talked about. It was always about something deeper and more meaningful. It didn't take much time to see that she walked to a different beat. It wasn't just what she wore or what she said but what she valued, which was more than surface things such as popularity or money. It didn't surprise me when I found out she was also an incredible artist.

Leah routinely asked me questions that gave me brief glimpses into how she saw and experienced the world. Questions like, "Have you ever been so struck with a beautiful sunset that you couldn't breathe?" "Has a budding flower ever made you cry?" "Have you ever woken up from a vivid dream where hundreds of lady bugs were crawling on one another and the picture in your head was so clear that you just had to paint it? My answer was always, "No. No, Leah, I have not."

On one occasion, Leah joined me to repaint the interior of our campus house. I had planned on putting something iconic on the front wall—something meaningful and unique but less traditional than a cross. I asked her what she thought, expecting it to be a casual conversation starter. Instead, she stopped what she was doing and just stared at the wall. She was envisioning something that would one day become our ministry logo. After a long and entranced moment, she broke the silence by asking me if I would let her paint the Trinity. *What?* I didn't even know how to explain the Trinity, how was she going to paint it? But that's what she did. She spent the next few weeks creating a beautiful mural. Amid an array of clouds, she painted a dove with an eight-foot wingspan holding a crown of thorns. It was amazing. Leah had a way of always bringing hidden spiritual realities into the open. She shined a light on the nature of God in ways that were fresh to everyone.

I've never known anyone who dreamt with the same intensity as Leah. As a student, she lived with Paulette and me for a short stint. It was not uncommon for her to wake up emotionally shook by what she had witnessed in a dream. Initially, I didn't pay much attention to her retellings over the breakfast table. But over time, it became clear that her dreams were different. She seemed to sense the spiritual undertow of things I could only see the surface of. Nothing highlighted this more than when she called me in December of 2019 saying, "I know this sounds weird, but I feel like we are about to experience a world-wide plague."

Experiences like this tend to reenforce a misperception that those with the gift of prophecy predict the future. However, if you were to ask Leah, she would say that the majority of what she hears from God has to do with the present, not the future. It's such present pressings of God that lead people like Leah to take action. In her case, it was the heartache she felt for the forgotten that later led her and her husband to adopt four multi-ethnic kids with special needs. Leah and I have remained friends over the years, and I routinely lean on her for spiritual insight. Her consistent and encouraging words have kept me grounded and encouraged through many turbulent seasons.

Those with the gift of prophesy shine a light not only on the heart of God but also on the hearts of people. That light can be encouraging, but it can also be convicting, which means a prophetic voice can seem strange and scary. I know that's how I initially felt around those with prophetic gifts. That's why I am forever grateful for a student named Christian, who helped me see the purpose of prophets more clearly.

Christian told me of a radical transformation during his high school years when he was brought into something called a "prophetic room." This terminology was new to me. It sounded weird so I was guarded. He described this prophetic room as a place where godly people prayed on his behalf and told him what God saw in his life. Their ability to shine light on his heart "wrecked" him—his word, not mine. I wasn't sure what to make of his experience, but there was no doubt he had good fruit in his life now.

He wanted the same "wrecking" for all those he loved in his life, and he requested that I send all my students and staff to a similar prophetic room. Of course, I couldn't do that. I didn't even know these people! But there was something about the sincerity of his request that struck me. Without really thinking about it, I blurted out that I would be willing to go myself. He was elated. I'll never forget his words as he left my office,

"You are not going to regret this. These are some heavy hitters!" *Oh, great. What does that mean?* I didn't know, but it sure felt like I was about to get wrecked.

As I drove about thirty minutes to the home where the meeting would take place, I became more and more uneasy. I felt like I was willingly walking into an ambush. I wondered if I was about to relive some of the bad experiences my students had encountered years ago. *What do I do if these people start barking like dogs?* Looking back, I don't know what kept me going. I was unprepared and completely at their mercy.

When I arrived, I was greeted by six people in a small living room. They explained that one person would pray silently throughout the evening as a way of covering us all with a blanket of peace. The rest would have their Bibles and ears open, tuning their senses to hear what God wanted to tell me.

What happened next really surprised me—the events that followed were not that weird at all. That's not to say what I experienced wasn't uniquely powerful and significant. It actually was an intense and meaningful experience, something I later heard described as "naturally supernatural." God was in that room, and the words shared were certainly anointed. These people had insight into parts of my life that could only have come from Jesus.

When the evening ended, I noticed that out of all the specifics they shared, none of them detailed any sin. I guess since I was expecting to be wrecked, I anticipated some dirt! So, I approached one of the women, cleared my throat, and said, "I noticed that everything you shared with me was positive. There was no mention of my many shortcomings. Only words of how God is really proud of me, notices my pure heart, and has big plans for me. I suppose as a minister, I'm an easy guy to encourage, but I'm curious as to what God says to the kid addicted to drugs and steeped in sin." The elderly woman leaned in, took my hand with two of hers, and patted them gently while saying, "Oh, sweetie. He tells them the same things."

That moment will stick with me forever. It showed me that our most significant wrecking is when we are wrecked by grace. That's when I really understood that what God sees in us is very different than what we assume he sees. What might our world look like if light was shown on all our hearts and what was revealed was nothing but how crazy God is for us? This is the role of our prophets, and we need to hear from them.

Could it be that you have this gift? Do you sometimes feel like God gives you special insight? Maybe you envision a picture like Leah or simply have a message to share. Do you ever feel like you are seeing something others don't? Do you seem to find yourself biting your lip for fear that your insight might be wrong? If you are gifted as a prophet, you have permission to live out your personal mission in light of this gift. Allow these words to be a message to you from Jesus. Let them rest on you with great gravity.

You are a heart revealer. Revealing the heart of God and the heart of people is vitally important. You use your light to expose the lies that accompany authority and power. You call us all to a better way. A harder way. You stand with the poor and the oppressed. You have an uncanny insight that reveals our core need for intimacy with God. God has made you a partner with the Holy Spirit. You are a guide to the committed and an agitator to the complacent. Now, go be you.

Evangelist: Illuminator of good news.

Evangelists are passionate about helping people see the gospel for what it is—good news. Biblically, the role of the evangelist is to share this good news. Nothing brings the evangelist more joy than to see someone's eyes light up as the things of God make sense to them for the first time. Evangelists have a way about them that puts others at ease. Evangelists tell stories that invite everyone into a common story. They radiate a love and sincerity that is noticed by all. Because of their loving transparency, they seem to get away with saying things that other people can't. Jon was just such a kid.

Jon was loved and respected by everyone in my ministry, by other students in his classes, and especially by other players on his baseball team. Jon was a gifted baseball player and showed a tremendous amount of loyalty to the team—the kind of loyalty that gave him a seat at the table with the partiers on the team as well as with those who spent all their time in the weight room. He fit in everywhere.

We all wanted Jon to succeed, and it seemed as if his time had come. It was the end of Jon's junior year, and he had just finished an incredible season. He was batting .400 in the highly competitive Missouri Valley baseball conference. We were all certain his dream of being drafted by a professional team was about to come true. When draft day came, his family and friends gathered for the big moment. Round one came and went. No call. It was a shock. What happened? Then round two. Still nothing. The entire day passed without a call. He later found out that his name had been removed from the list by people who wanted him back for his senior year. It was devastating. It's hard to imagine anyone responding to this news with anything less than a vengeful lawsuit. But that's not what Jon did.

There was something about the experience that woke Jon from his spiritual slumber. He quickly shifted from self-pity to wondering how he might leverage this new challenge for good. He told me he felt like this was God's way of allowing him to accomplish some unfinished business. He loved his teammates and felt that each of them deserved to know how the good news of Jesus pertained to their situation.

The following year, the first thing he did was leverage his status as a captain so he could room with a different teammate on every road trip. This was the perfect setting to talk about the good news one-on-one. Never before had these guys heard someone outside of church talk about God the way Jon did. And it didn't feel like Jon was preaching at them. There was no pretension or arrogance in Jon's message; just good news. To Jon, this was simple. It was as if he'd found gas for .99 cents a gallon. What kind of friend would he be if he didn't pass that good news along to his friends?

Unfortunately, sharing good news isn't how evangelism is typically perceived by Christians. In fact, the view of evangelism is often so negative that many evangelists initially don't even want to believe they have this gift. They have wrongfully adopted the idea that evangelism is synonymous with being heavy-handed and condemning. This couldn't be further from the truth. True evangelists are instinctively relatable and unoffensive. They share in a way that comes straight from the heart and puts people at ease.

It was Jon's honest and humble approach that illuminated the gospel and ultimately led his best friend—who was also the biggest partier on the team—to accept this good news and be baptized. Seeing a life transform right before his eyes, catalyzed a personal mission within Jon. This mission was solidified a few months later, when Jon's words lit up the gospel again. This time, thirty young men surrendered to Jesus on a softball diamond before a game. Jon never did get drafted onto a professional baseball team, but his course was set. He chose to fully pursue his personal mission, which eventually led him to start one of the fastest growing churches in Chicago called Mission Church.

The evangelist's ability to listen and empathize is what makes their presentation of the gospel message so relevant. It's the evangelist who helps us remember that the gospel is multifaceted. Yes, Jesus dying in our stead and offering us eternity in heaven is the crown jewel of good news. However, remembering that Jesus is also the healer of broken relationships, the provider in stark circumstances, and the restorer of purposeful lives is the kind of practical good news that makes the gospel relevant and compelling.

Here's another characteristic of evangelists that seems especially significant for the times in which we live: they have unifying power. In a culture that is divided and hyperpolarized, we need evangelists to shine their light on something bigger and higher than left and right agendas. We need a few brave souls to unite us around a bigger ideal. I deeply appreciate the evangelistic work of leaders such as Andy Stanley, who leverage their lives outside of the church as well as within it. It's in our schools, businesses, and politics that we need more leaders who are willing to stand in the middle, get shot from both sides, and shine their light on the good news we all want to live. In seasons of conflict, it's imperative that we rally around our common values. It's the evangelist who has the ability to communicate these commonalities better than anyone else.

So how about you? Do you find yourself frustrated when good news is presented in ways that are unnecessarily complex? Do you have an instinctive ability to contextualize the gospel for a variety of audiences? Does the gospel seem to always be both at the surface, ready to be shared, and simultaneously residing deep at your core? Are you frustrated that sharing the good news is perceived as a special ability that only a few possess, believing that everyone should be doing the same?

Perhaps the power of your personal mission has been muted by the cultural pressures around you. If so, allow Jesus to launch you into a fresh season in which, you have permission to freely share the good news. Let these be his words to you.

You are a storyteller. You use your light to feature the greatest story ever told. You help everyone understand how all lives belong under God's grand umbrella of grace. You have a knack for inviting people into the kingdom because you naturally speak many contextual languages. You also excite and invigorate the people of God to find their own voices as ambassadors for the kingdom. Mostly, you care about good news being articulated clearly for as many people as possible to hear. You are infectious. People readily trust you. Your very lifestyle is a form of hospitality. God has made you a recruiter for the good, glorious, and adventurous life. Now, go be you.

Shepherd: Illuminator of the people around you.

Biblically speaking, shepherds care for the flock. In the same way that shepherds care for sheep in the fold, spiritual shepherds care for the people within the church. Everyone loves a shepherd. What's not to love?

They keep us cared for and protected. Their passion is creating a sense of belonging, and they are fueled by relationships.

Shepherds believe in their core that everyone is important, and they are committed to shining their light on the lives of the oppressed and forgotten. The effectiveness of a good shepherd is directly proportionate to the amount of time they spend with those they care for. There is no substitute for time. The old adage is true: people don't care how much you know until they know how much you care. Consequently, shepherding is one of those gifts all of us can practice simply by increasing our availability. However, those who have the gift of shepherding bring to it an innate depth and sincerity that no one taught them—it's just who they are.

Polly was one such person in my student ministry. She was on the university diving team, and she cared deeply for her coaches and teammates. The long hours spent at the pool wore thin for some, but Polly loved having the opportunity to shine her light on those who meant so much to her. Polly was highly principled and made it clear that she was a Christian, but nothing about the way she lived her faith was obnoxious or turned people off. Instead, she lived her faith by modeling integrity and consistency every day. Polly was known to ask lots of questions and listen intently to the answers. I can always tell when someone is a shepherd by the way they empathetically engage with the person in front of them, regardless of how popular that person might be. I've noticed over the years that shepherds have this innate ability to listen with their eyes. It's a beautiful feeling to know that you are the focal point of a shepherd's attention.

Over time, Polly invited one of her teammates to her small-group Bible study. The girl accepted her invitation and assumed a priest would be attending as well. This mental picture of a priest sitting cross-legged in her apartment still cracks me up. Not wanting to draw attention to herself, Polly decided to let her teammate naturally discover that this meeting would actually be led by her. Polly spent a lot of time preparing for the meeting. She baked, cleaned, and prayed. And she put thought into how

PART 2   PERMISSION TO BE ARMED AND DANGEROUS: DEVELOPING HOLY VALOR

her teammate, who had little to no experience studying the Bible, might feel as the evening unfolded. To keep her friend from the embarrassment of not knowing how to find the Scripture passage they were studying, Polly thoughtfully placed a bookmark in the passage ahead of time. This small gesture made a big impact on her teammate, and no one else in the group ever picked up on her subtle aid. It wasn't meant for them.

I'm sure the rest of the evening went well. I'm confident the environment was pleasant, the company was kind, and the study was significant. But it's the quiet details of thoughtful intentionality that sometimes make the biggest difference. That's when recipients of a shepherd's attention discover they have benefited from a light intended only for them. The bookmark was just one of many ways Polly let her friend know she was seen. Even though her teammate didn't decide to follow Christ that year, Polly remained a faithful friend even after she graduated. Polly never saw her friend as a project; she saw her only as a person, and she did her best to model the life of Jesus. Over time, it was Polly's unconditional and persistent love that guided her friend into her own long-lasting relationship with Jesus. Even after graduation, Polly remained available to talk, laugh, and cry. And a year later, she drove hours back to campus to join her teammate's baptism party.

In addition to shining their light on those who might be overlooked or forgotten, shepherds are also known for their keen awareness of threats. When a shepherd senses danger for the community, they can be very protective. The shepherd's sensitivity to the marginalized can ignite a fury in them when those they love are threatened. Shepherds have an uncanny ability to sniff out dangerous people with ulterior motives. They can sense financial, physical, and sexual threats well before others. There is nothing that will transform a shepherd from a soft-spoken and gentle presence into a furious fighter more quickly than the threat of an outsider.

Of all the gifts, shepherding seems to be most synonymous with discipleship. There is no substitute for giving others the gift of time when it comes to practicing the discipleship that Jesus modeled. Whether it's book studies, breakfasts, or late-night discussions, time intentionally leveraged is how disciples are made. So, whether or not we have a natural propensity toward shepherding, spending intentional time with people is a discipline we should all develop. In fact, to develop a personal mission beyond the walls of church, I'm convinced we must develop, at least on some level, the practice of shepherding. However, to be clear, there is a difference between developing shepherding skills and having the gift of shepherding. True shepherds have a selfless sincerity that those around them can feel. These gifted souls just have a way of blocking out distractions while tuning their ears and eyes to the one in front of them. They make those they shepherd feel like they are the only ones in the room.

To be on the receiving end of attention from a shepherd is not to feel exposed, but to feel seen and appreciated. It's this sort of unconditional friendship that produces the healthiest versions of ourselves. In a way, it's the shepherds who develop the gifts of those around them.

If you are a shepherd, know that you play a crucial role in advancing the kingdom. It's your attentive eyes and ears that allow those closest to you to feel seen and heard. Big things are cultivated within small circles, and that's your superpower. Cultural anthropologist Margaret Mead once said, "Never doubt that a small group of thoughtful, committed citizens can change the world; indeed, it's the only thing that ever has." The care and attention you give to those within your circle is likely all that's needed to catalyze multiple personal missions around you. As you devote yourself to speaking life into those who may feel forgotten, know that *you* are not forgotten. You are seen, you are valued, and you are needed. In this moment, allow Jesus to be your shepherd, the one who longs to care for you. Let these words resonate deep within you.

You are a soul healer. You leverage your light to reveal that all God's people are unique and precious. You guard the community from wolves as you guide them toward still waters. You believe community should be a healing environment, a place where we work through past hurts while collectively becoming people of wholeness. Every individual is important to you. You readily invest time and show interest while exhibiting a spirit that is warmly present. You create environments in which people feel safe enough to be vulnerable. God has made you to be relational glue. Now, go be you.

Teacher: Illuminator of the Word of God.

Biblically speaking, much like shepherds, teachers care for members within the church. Unlike the apostles, prophets, and evangelists, whose ministries are largely directed to unbelievers, the ministry of teachers is directed toward believers. Teachers shine their light on the source of light, God's Word, which King David described as a lamp for our feet and a light for our path (Psalm 119:10). Teachers understand that God's Word is a trustworthy light that exposes darkness and provides guidance to all who submit to it. Teachers have a passion for truth, and they know there is nothing more foundational and authoritative than the Bible. It's their resilient commitment to the truth that keeps the bedrock of our ministries stable and credible.

Teaching God's Word is a gift reserved for a few. The apostle James states, "*Not many of you should become teachers*" (James 3:1 niv). And we followed that directive in our campus ministry, focusing instead on cultivating self-discovery environments. So, it wasn't until I met a guy named Eric that I experienced firsthand the powerful contribution of those with a teaching gift.

Eric was in his late thirties and a nontraditional student at a nearby Christian college. He was a teacher through and through and had been taking college courses for almost twenty years. Eric was also the first person I met who wasn't in school to chase a degree. He was chasing knowledge. When he and his study partner decided to change up their location one evening, they stopped by our campus house. While there, they overheard some of my students asking sincere questions about the Bible. Instead of being judgmental of this student ministry that apparently wasn't providing answers, Eric was invigorated to learn there was such a place that had spiritually hungry people in it.

Eric approached me the next day with great humility and requested to be a resource for the ministry. I readily accepted, and it began a beautiful relationship that I hold dear to this day. I've learned a lot from Eric, and he would say he's learned a lot from me. We concluded that we both valued knowledge but followed different paths to find it. Mine was through life and ministry experience, and his was through books. I can't tell you how many times he shared a new thought from his reading that paralleled a truth that had taken me lots of trial and error to figure out. He was my book filter. He would wade through a stack of books and then tell me which chapters were relevant to what I needed to hear at the time. Eric helped me in other practical ways as well. Remember the run-in I had with the people who were consumed with the manifestation of spiritual gifts? And do you remember the epic Scripture throwdown that ended the debate? Yeah, that was Eric. He was the Yin to my Yang. The teacher to my apostle. We made a great team, and it was wonderful.

As time went on, I realized that my teaching wasn't really teaching; it was preaching. I cared about truth, but with my apostleship nature, I was more concerned about using truth as a catalyst toward taking new kingdom ground. I decided that our ministry needed a teacher as well, so I asked Eric to lead a midweek Bible study. And part of what made Eric such a brilliant teacher was that he asked far more questions than he provided answers. In fact, it's been my experience that the Word of God shines brightest and does its best work in environments that are leaderless. It's in these self-reflective spaces that the Spirit of God becomes our teacher. Eric showed me the importance of teaching people how to teach themselves. He was constantly showing all of us how to do our own research, how to cross-reference verses, and how to use a Greek lexicon. Eric was a true teacher. He understood that within Christian culture, especially the celebrity aspect of it, it was far too common to see teachers elevated to a place of authority that undermined our personal reliance on the Word. If the aftereffects of a teacher's message create more dependence on the teacher (rather than God's Word), the teacher hasn't done his or her job well. The apostle Paul affirms that we should all learn to teach ourselves:

> In fact, though by this time you ought to be teachers, you need someone to teach you the elementary truths of God's word all over again. You need milk, not solid food! Anyone who lives on milk, being still an infant, is not acquainted with the teaching about righteousness. But solid food is for the mature, who by constant use have trained themselves to distinguish good from evil. (Hebrews 5:12-14 NIV)

Paul is frustrated that people are not maturing. He's calling them babies. He suggests that if we want to be mature, we must train ourselves. If we don't learn to feed ourselves, we become perpetual infants who never stop breastfeeding.

Learning from Eric's example made me rethink what I'd always understood to be good teaching. No matter how deep a teaching may be, if it is always spoon-fed to me, then it is still milk. If we are always waiting to be fed, we are the equivalent of baby birds with mouths wide open, never leaving the nest.

Perhaps you are a teacher who longs to uphold the truth. Maybe, you have been sidelined because there appear to be so few outlets to practice your gift. Be assured that Jesus has a role for you. He has words of encouragement to share with you. Let this commissioning fill you with confidence that allows you to create your own opportunities and to pursue your unique and God-given personal mission.

You are a light giver. You illuminate the Word and help people understand it in a life-giving way. You have an insatiable appetite for learning. You care about accuracy, accumulate knowledge, distribute wisdom, and demonstrate maturity. You masterfully point people to a trustworthy source of productive self-discovery without being a distraction. God has made you to be a guardian of truth and to uphold all that is reliable and accurate. Now, go be you.

Your Most Important Discovery of All

Now that I've spent years helping hundreds of people discover their spiritual gifts, I've concluded that just as important as discovering the gifts we have is discovering the gifts we don't have. This understanding will prove helpful later as we explore our permission to start fires in Part 4.

As a leader, I've witnessed the profound beauty of watching people identify and appreciate the gifts in other people, which is why I discourage people from taking online spiritual gifts assessments. Instead, it is a necessary and more profound experience to receive affirmation and input from the lips of those who know you best. Plus, if we fail to appreciate those who are different than us, we will inevitably surround ourselves only with people who are gifted in the same ways we are. This severely limits the full expression of the kingdom of heaven here on earth. For example, instead of working hard to experience the beautiful balance of all five gifts working together, we might find it far easier to migrate to a church that only honors the gift(s) we are comfortable with. Teachers congregating together to form Bible churches or prophets gathering to form charismatic churches, to name a few.

To develop a personal mission beyond the church walls, you will not only need to identify your own spiritual gift but will also need to develop a keen eye for recognizing and honoring the gifts of those around you. The practice of encouraging others will give you perspective and help you see how all the gifts work together. If we believe that Jesus' intent was to establish his kingdom on earth, then we must practice a personal mission that makes room for everyone. The following is intended to help you bring the gifts within the people around you to life.

Apostle. Who do you know who is always dreaming? Who never tires of experimentation. Who sees new opportunities where others see only dead ends?

Respect the apostles around you. Ask them what their big idea is. (They have one). Be quick to say, "Wow!" and slow to say, "How?" A simple acknowledgement from you may be all it takes to launch the next great expansion of the kingdom.

Prophet. Who do you know who has their ears tuned to God in a unique way? Who sees what God sees and feels what God sees and feels? Who do you trust to tell you the truth, even when it hurts?

Honor the prophets around you. Routinely ask them what they are feeling and noticing. Young prophets, especially, can be hesitant to speak for fear of being wrong. God's message to his people may be on the tip of someone's tongue standing in your circle.

Evangelist. Who are the storytellers in your midst? Who knows how to intuitively share the gospel in a variety of environments? Who has a voice that just seems to carry further than most?

Emulate the evangelists around you. Encourage them to speak. Our culture in and out of church has shamed evangelists into silence. Be their cheerleader. Follow their lead. Nothing will encourage an evangelist more than applying their passion to sharing good news.

Shepherd. Who do you know who listens with their eyes? Who asks you the questions about your life you hope someone will ask? Who seems to always have time for you, even when they don't? These are probably the shepherds in your life.

Relieve the shepherds around you. Don't take all their time. Rather, ask them who they wish they had more time for. Find ways to invest in those people.

Teacher. Who do you know who has an insatiable appetite for learning? Who cares about accuracy and reliability? Who believes they are sidelined because the "official" teaching positions are filled?

Develop the teachers around you. Ask them to help you with difficult questions. Encourage them to teach people how to teach themselves.

PART 3

PERMISSION TO FLIP THE SCRIPT: DEVELOPING A NEW SEQUENCE OF ORDER

We cannot solve our problems with the same thinking we used when we created them.
—Albert Einstein

To develop a godly personal mission, we need to resist the temptation to succumb to what I refer to as an "established order." An established order is essentially the accepted status quo; it's what we have collectively come to believe is the best way of doing things. We tend to forget that Jesus was always flipping the script and upending the status quo. Instead of being served by the disciples, he washed their feet; instead of dining with the religious leaders, he ate with sinners; instead of building an empire, he released a movement. I admit, established orders have their place. They are predictable and logical. The problem comes when we equate their predictability and logic with God's ways.

God's ways are rarely predictable or logical by human standards. When we are pursuing dreams that originate with God, it only stands to reason that our path might look somewhat different than the status quo. Jesus always seemed to live in a way that countered the logic of the world. The life he modeled for us was fully successful at achieving his mission, yet his game plan was also consistently backward from what anyone at the time would have expected. The apostle Paul explained it like this: "For the foolishness of God is wiser than human wisdom, and the weakness of God is stronger than human strength" (1 Corinthians 1:25).

Throughout Scripture, God consistently used weak people and backward game plans to accomplish his work. You don't have to look very hard to see that Jesus flipped the script at almost every opportunity. Although he was a king, he arrived on earth as a baby, worked as a carpenter, ministered as a servant, and died as a criminal. And throughout his ministry, he flipped the script on everything we've come to equate with success. So, the question we need to ask is: *What does that mean for us and how do we pursue our personal mission?* It means we have permission to flip the script as well.

I had an opportunity to flip the script when I resigned from the campus ministry position I'd held for twenty-two years. It was all I knew. And yet, it was this unsettling transition that gave me the courage to look at my personal mission from a fresh angle. I knew I had a lot to learn and a lot to let go of. If I was going to gain a fresh outlook, it would require yet another getaway. Another intentional launch time with God. This time, the launching pad was a much different location than a retreat center or the front seat of a car. Through the generosity of my brother, I had the opportunity to camp on an island in Ontario, Canada. For nearly two weeks, I was surrounded by nature, with no distractions and no time constraints. My intent for this secluded getaway was to discover what God wanted me to do for the second half of my personal mission here on earth. I wanted to examine my life without considering the expectations of my supporters, staff members, or board. My plan was to set aside everything I had previously known and look at the Scriptures as if I'd never seen them before. I was ready to flip the script.

While sitting on that island, I read through the gospel stories of Jesus, as I'd done many times before. But this time, I read with a different intent.

As I read through these biographies of Jesus' life, I set aside the lessons he taught—something I'd been trained to look for—and instead looked more intently at his approach. Basically, I honed in on the method of his ministry. My discoveries were more profound than I even anticipated. Jesus was consistently flipping the script. As I studied, I began to notice a pattern that I organized into five categories—five ways in which Jesus worked backward from the established order that surrounded him. In his ministry, Jesus consistently chose:

- Being before doing
- Chaos before order
- Self-discovery before formal teaching
- Time before invitation
- Authority before assignment

After returning home, I focused my studies on the gospel movements currently active worldwide. That's when I made another profound discovery. It turns out that these five patterns Jesus modeled were also the skeletal structure of every major God movement in the world. And yet, of the 900-plus large-scale gospel movements that were currently happening throughout the world, none were in the United States. Could it be that our American version of church has its roots too deeply embedded in the Christian status quo? Could it be that other nations, especially impoverished ones, have found something we can't see? Could it be that as we develop our personal mission, we, too, need to flip the script?

In this section, we'll explore each of the five patterns Jesus used to flip the script in pursuit of his mission. As we do so, I'll be introducing you to some of the most heroic people I know. People who understand that holding tight to Jesus means having the courage to flip the script. It's these examples that have led me smack dab in the center of some of the most beautifully backward circumstances I've ever found myself in. As you read these stories, I hope it will become evident that with each season and each relationship, you too, have permission to flip the script as you pursue your God-given mission.

PART 3 PERMISSION TO FLIP THE SCRIPT: DEVELOPING A NEW SEQUENCE OF ORDER

6. BEING BEFORE DOING

There was one class I took while attending a small Bible college that taught me more than all the other classes I took combined. Dr. Brant Lee Doty, the professor for that class, had been among the founding fathers of the college. In his prime, he was one of the brightest scholars the school had ever known. But by the time I was in my senior year, his standing had diminished. Age had caught up with him, and dementia had set in. As a token of appreciation for his many years of faithful service, he was given a small office on campus. He had no official responsibilities except to teach one class on the Book of Hebrews. I have no idea who decided to allow him to teach, but I thank them.

I signed up for his class and arrived on the first day to discover that there were just two students—me and a young woman, whose name I can no longer recall. But I can still remember Dr. Doty's first lecture. Despite the intimate setting, Dr. Doty chose to stand tall at the front of the class as if addressing a packed lecture hall. He was dressed in a three-piece suit. He stood behind the lectern, cleared his throat a few times, and then uttered his first words bold and clear: "Hebrews, chapter one."

What he shared next was nothing short of brilliant. It was content I'd never heard before. It was so good that I awkwardly asked the girl next to me for a pen. Being that there were only two of us, it was a risky move that could have disrupted the flow of the moment. But I didn't have to worry about breaking Dr. Doty's rhythm—not today anyway; he was on a roll, and we all knew it. The only question was whether I could take notes fast enough to capture it. I was a terrible student and wasn't used to taking notes, but there was something about the power of Dr. Doty's words that compelled me to try.

Before I knew it, the class was over, and this girl and I looked at each other in astonishment and appreciation for what we had just experienced. I suppose part of our fascination was tied to our low expectations. We both knew of his dementia, and we were happy just to be part of what seemed to have been one of his good days.

The next class didn't start quite as well. He was late, and we both knew why. He had forgotten. I suppose we could have ignored it and gone on with our day, but we were both hungry for more. So, I decided to go get him. As I approached his office, I could tell he had no idea he was supposed to be teaching.

"Hey, Doc," I said. "Can I walk you to class today?" The reminder prompted him, as I hoped it would.

"Oh, yes. Yes, of course," he said. "Let me just grab my things." He picked up his notebook and Bible, and off we went.

This was clearly not one of his good days. I felt badly for him, especially when his first words were once again, "Hebrews, chapter one." *Oh, no. Was he really going to repeat himself?* The answer was yes and no. I'm sure he fully believed he was teaching Hebrews 1 for the first time, but the content was still rich and full of things that were missing from the first lecture. I was astounded. Once again, I borrowed a pen and took notes.

This was the pattern for the next several weeks. I walked Dr. Doty to class, and he taught on Hebrews 1. Every. Single. Week. And here's the craziest part. I took notes. Every. Single. Week. All these years later, I can't remember much of what I wrote down, but the lesson that has stuck with me to this day is that Dr. Doty taught from a place of being. No matter how much his brain failed him, his soul was full, and there was always something fresh that came from it. I decided that year that I, too, wanted to live a life that overflowed from my being. There is just nothing that compares to a life that draws from a deeper well.

Being

Here is the foundational idea when it comes to being: *You cannot share what you do not have.* Regardless of the unique mission God has for you, you are not fully equipped for that mission until you first possess what people need. In other words, you need to be a firsthand recipient of the grace you offer. If not, you're merely peddling a product.

It's a bit of a mystery that I can't fully explain, but when we are transformed by Jesus through a posture of surrender, people seem to notice. It's as if they have a radar that detects whether they are being offered a treasure or a sales pitch. If we reduce even the greatest news in the world to a statement, we believe but do not live; we rob the gospel of its power. The truth we share must be accompanied by a life that is healthy and renewed if we hope to see its power transform others. Sure, Dr. Doty shared incredible statements of gospel truth, but it was the transformed quality of his life that gave credibility to all he said. It was clear he tapped into a power source I desperately wanted to tap into. This is what distinguishes a God-given personal mission from all the rest. God's mission is always accompanied by a deep and fulfilling life, one sustained by a power source Jesus called living water.

> Jesus stood and shouted to the crowds, "Anyone who is thirsty may come to me! Anyone who believes in me may come and drink! For the Scriptures declare, 'Rivers of living water will flow from his heart.'" (John 7:37-38 NLT)

Conversely, when we try to share the gospel by giving cognitive answers alone, we have nothing refreshing to offer. We may have every intention of sharing living water, but until we are first transformed by the real thing, we have little more to offer than a study on H2O. The information we share might be true, but it lacks power.

Doing

If *being* is the process by which we become the gospel, *doing* is how we live it out. When it comes to carrying out our personal mission, being isn't enough. We also need to do something. However, the first step of action is not intuitive. Fortunately, Jesus perfectly modeled this God-dependent backward way. Before he acted, he prayed. He was always praying. He prayed before traveling to the next town. He prayed before going to the cross. He prayed before selecting the twelve disciples. And let's not forget that he started his ministry with forty days of prayer and fasting. Jesus was intentional about keeping in step with his Father. He knew that regular conversation with his Father would keep him from acting too fast or too soon and suffering the consequences.

Acting too soon is something I struggle with. When I get excited about an idea, I want to act on it *now*. As someone with the gift of apostleship, I come by that naturally, but some of it can also be attributed to immaturity. Over the years, I've needed to set aside my eagerness and admit that my mission won't disappear by waiting on God; in fact, it will come into greater focus.

However, there is also a danger in waiting too long. We will never feel as ready for action as we'd like, but we also can't stay in prayer mode forever. This is the tension especially, when we're taking a risk to do something we haven't done before. But we must move forward. Fast or slow, one thing is certain: God will likely move in a way that forces us to adjust to him, not the other way around.

So how about you? Do you wish you had more certainty about the next steps you need to take to pursue your mission? Maybe this is a new area for you, and as much as you'd like to keep pace with God, you really don't know how. If so, there is a simple step you can take as a starting point. It's called a prayer walk, and as I've come to discover, it's a proven tool practiced around the world.

PART 3 PERMISSION TO FLIP THE SCRIPT: DEVELOPING A NEW SEQUENCE OF ORDER

Prayer Walk

A prayer walk is simply an intentional walk with God. You choose an area—your neighborhood, your kids' school, a dilapidated section of town—and go for a walk with God. Prayer walks are a practical way for God to help us find tangible outlets for our personal mission. When we get outside and look around, God helps us recognize and engage with the needs in our community. This simple exercise also helps us see that everything God cares about tends to fall into one of three categories: people, places, and problems. As you walk, look around and ask God questions like these: What are the needs of the *people* I see? What should be added or detracted to make this *place* flourish? What is the glaring *problem or the first domino that needs to fall in order to bring substantial change?* It's this practice of getting outside and seeing what God sees that can lead us to adjust our personal mission to meet the most foundational needs and address the core problems of those around us.

Prayer walks help us see what God sees and feel what God feels. They are God's way of nudging us outside, where we might bump into neighbors, discover that abandoned building downtown, or stumble on that problem of the unsupervised kids at the end of the street. When we obey Jesus, even in the small rhythms of prayer, there is a good chance that something will break our heart and move us to action.

Jesus did this all the time. He understood how essential it was to get out of his current surroundings and see the world through God's eyes. Sometimes, Jesus' walks led him to people, such as a hurting and forgotten woman at a well. Another time, he ministered to an unredeemed place named Caesarea Philippi. And then there was the time he solved the large problem of feeding more than 5,000 hungry people. In short, Jesus was always reaching out to people, places, and problems.

Our personal mission should be no different. When we take our prayer walks with God, we look around while asking him what people are hurting, what places need to be redeemed, and what problems need to be resolved.

Although it wasn't clear to me at the time, I can now see that the modesty Dr. Doty displayed in his classroom all those years ago was more than an admirable characteristic in his old age. It was also the fuel that empowered him to do great things, like start a Bible college. His life accomplishments demand that we see him as more than a kind old man. He was a living example of flipping the script in multiple facets of his life. Facets that, as we will see next, were far from modest, reserved, or predictable.

PART 3 PERMISSION TO FLIP THE SCRIPT: DEVELOPING A NEW SEQUENCE OF ORDER

7. CHAOS BEFORE ORDER

On our tenth wedding anniversary, we went on our first and only cruise. Never had I experienced the joy of unpacking once and letting my hotel transport me about—and through the islands of the Caribbean no less!

Everything was taken care of. There were housekeeping attendants to tidy up, chefs to prepare food, and entertainment at every turn. I loved how orderly it all was. Unlike other vacations, I didn't have to figure out where to eat, arrange a tour, or set up a tee time. The staff on the cruise ship took care of everything.

One of my favorite parts of cruise life is when the ship stops at different ports along the way. Usually, there are a couple excursions to choose from, or you can simply sit at the beach. When I noticed that one of our upcoming stops was in Haiti, I was both puzzled and intrigued. Given what I knew about the intense poverty of Haiti, I had a hard time seeing how stopping there would fit with what I knew about cruise culture. So, I figured I would at least get off the ship, stretch my legs, and explore a bit.

When the boat docked and I got to the beach, I was taken aback. This didn't look like Haiti at all. It was nice, *really nice*—as in a white sand beach with lounge chairs and a Mai Tai bar. What was most surprising, however, was what was *not* there. Up and down the beach, as far as the eye could see, there were no Haitians. None. Then I spotted something most everyone else didn't see, or at least didn't want to see. It was a fence covered with foliage—a fence that hid the less presentable parts of Haiti from view and allowed the paying customers to experience a cruise version of Haiti for the next few hours.

I decided I wanted to see more, so I walked along the beach looking for breaks in the fence. Finally, I found a spot where the vegetation was not so overgrown. As I got closer, I could see there was a gate, and sitting on the other side were two little girls who were no older than six or seven. They sat close and held one another tightly. They were wearing mismatched, torn clothes, and the dirt on their cute little faces highlighted their big brown eyes that were now locked with mine. They looked as if they'd been caught doing something wrong, but they didn't run.

I wanted to connect in some way, but quickly discerned there was nothing I could do. Here I was, a white, well-dressed man who spoke a different language and came from that big boat. I couldn't help but think about how much fun these girls could have on the boat. There was a pool, games, and all the ice cream they could eat. But I realized that even if it had been possible to bring them on for a bit, and assuming that I could communicate the invitation clearly, there is no way they would. They knew they didn't belong there. It wasn't their place.

I'm afraid many of us churchgoers have become something like cruise people. We've been going to our orderly church for thirty years or more and can't see how what we have grown to love, may not be what other people love, or even need. As hard as it may be for us to accept, there are many people in our communities who will never see our church as *their* place. And the more time we spend with the people on our ship, the more blinded we will become to anything other than our own culture.

Repetition over time will only deepen our conditioned biases'. I can still remember getting back on the cruise liner and overhearing a well-intentioned but misguided woman who was on her twenty-fourth cruise. I knew this was her twenty-fourth cruise because, like many of the other guests, she repeatedly announced, "By the way, did you know that this was my twenty-fourth cruise?" What came out of her mouth next brought this unfortunate parallel to church full circle.

"I love Haiti," she said.

Really? I thought. *Does she even realize that what she just experienced on the beach was fiction created for tourists?*

"If they would let me, I would love to pay for a couple of Haitians to go on a cruise themselves," she added.

She assumed she knew Haiti because of what she'd seen of it on the beach. She also believed she knew what Haitians really needed and wanted—the same consumer experience she had come to love. So, as we're developing our personal mission, how do we keep ourselves from falling into the same trap, of thinking we already have or know what everyone else needs? It's a monumental mistake to assume the only answer to the chaos of our world is provided by our version of order. We need to enter the chaos by becoming students, not a teachers, and a guests rather than a hosts.

Be a Student, not a Teacher

Too often, we assume that our job as Christians is to rescue people from their context by bringing them into ours instead of taking the good news into theirs. We think what they need is what we have. But what if our first steps of engagement had less to do with what we have to offer and more to do with learning their names and discovering their needs? Doesn't that sound more appealing, and maybe even exciting?

People love to be known, and they love to be asked. When you enter the chaos of a new territory as a student rather than a teacher, you are in the perfect posture for God to use you. When you first learn about the needs of that school, neighborhood, or workplace, you create bonds of trust that provide a natural way for people to see the practical and helpful side of Jesus' kingdom. This is how God does his best work! It's only with this frame of mind that we begin to see that what those two little girls and their families needed most was not a few hours on a cruise ship, but maybe a school, a hospital, or even a home.

Instead of assuming that the work God has for you is about bringing as many people as possible into your church, consider whether God is inviting you to spend more time with people who may never attend your church. Think about how you can be a student of the territory God leads you to and how you might contextualize Jesus' good news to meet the most pressing needs you discover. Contextualizing good news requires a commitment to being a humble student of the story within that context and culture. And one of the best ways to do that is to be the guest of an insider, someone who already belongs there.

Be a Guest, not a Host

Have you ever noticed that Jesus was never a host? Instead, as a guest, he ate at Matthew's house with tax collectors and sinners. It was at Simon the leper's house that he encountered the poor woman who poured perfume on his head. And when he was approached by a desperately seeking man named Zacchaeus, he insisted that they go to his house. Jesus never tried to take people out of their chaos; instead, as a guest, always entered the mess. He never shied away from nasty, polluted, and chaotic places. As demonstrated by the woman at the well in Samaria, the dirtier the place, the better. One of my good friends says that the most beautiful things grow best out of fertilizer. Jesus understood this, and we must too. He prayed for God's kingdom to come to earth as it is in heaven. If we want to see the kingdom of heaven saturate the kingdom of earth, it must migrate from chaos to order. Not the other way around. Church membership transfers were never in Jesus' plan. He went to the nooks and crannies of his society and taught his disciples to do the same.

In Matthew 10 and Luke 10, Jesus sends His disciples into new places but cautions them to not enter a house that doesn't first have a "worthy person," or in some translations, a "person of peace." He understood how important it was to ride on the coattails of an insider as you go—to have someone who can vouch for you. It's the practice of finding a good host who has already established relational equity with the people in that community. They are the gatekeepers. Doesn't it make more sense to find gatekeepers instead of spending years trying to become one? Doesn't it sound more appealing and effective to find one peacemaker than to win over a crowd? This is exactly what Jesus did in one of the most difficult environments of His time.

> Now he had to go through Samaria. So, he came to a town in Samaria called Sychar, near the plot of ground Jacob had given to his son Joseph. Jacob's well was there, and Jesus, tired as he was from the journey, sat down by the well. It was about noon. When a Samaritan woman came to draw water, Jesus said to her, "Will you give me a drink?" (John 4:4–7 NIV)

For a Jew, there was no culture messier or more deplorable than that of the Samaritans. Samaritans were considered the lowest of the low-unfit to be firewood for hell! The disdain was so great that Jews refused to even walk in their region. They intentionally walked around Samaria so as to not interact. That's what makes Jesus' action here so profound: not only did He go through Samaria, but he insisted on being their guest. The text says that *he had to go* through Samaria, and once there, he asked the woman at the well for a drink.

So where do you *have to go*? What part of town is continually calling your name? What group of people is drawing you in? As a means of giving them dignity, what can you ask of them? The answer to these questions may not be on the tip of your tongue, but they will come with each intentional step you take into chaos. I don't think God is concerned that you don't yet know who you will meet. I don't think he is waiting for your personal mission to be fully developed. He will work that out on the fly. He just needs your willingness to be a student and a guest in a new territory. And chances are good that the host you find will be unlike *anyone* you might expect. But riding on the coattails of someone well-known in that context will bring about results unlike *anything* you might expect. In Jesus' case, even the town tramp brought about a bigger result than he could bring himself.

[28] Then, leaving her water jar, the woman went back to the town and said to the people, [29] "Come, see a man who told me everything I ever did. Could this be the Messiah?" [30] They came out of the town and made their way toward him.

[39] Many of the Samaritans from that town believed in him because of the woman's testimony, "He told me everything I ever did."

There may be times to invite people to your church on Sunday, but if we are going to develop a personal mission beyond the walls of church, we need to get comfortable with the idea of being guests. Aligning with hosts who serve as gatekeepers has always been Jesus' way to bring good news to the world. This, too, is our calling. Whether it's to the skateboard park down the street or into the break room at work, good news best travels through established hosts who can speak the contextual language of the people. Sometimes, that's a prestigious and well-respected person. Sometimes, it's the town prostitute. And sometimes, it may just be two little girls with dirty faces.

PART 3 PERMISSION TO FLIP THE SCRIPT: DEVELOPING A NEW SEQUENCE OF ORDER

8. SELF-DISCOVERY BEFORE FORMAL TEACHING

There is little debate that the most powerful form of learning is self-discovery. Nothing compares to those "aha" moments when the veil suddenly lifts from our eyes and we see with clarity that which was hidden just moments before. What we learn through self-discovery is memorable and often becomes the bedrock for ongoing learning. One of the things I've learned over the years is that it is questions, not statements, that best facilitate self-discovery. This is important because an essential part of every personal mission is helping people experience "aha" moments about Jesus and life in his kingdom. We might think that requires a lot of formal teaching—transferring the information we have about God to those who don't yet have it—but is that how God usually works? Think about your own experience. When did God speak loudest? My guess is that it was in silence, not a sermon, and while sitting with a question, not a statement.

While formal teaching is essential, self-discovery is always the best starting point, and that's what makes asking questions such a powerful strategy. Learning how to leverage questions for self-discovery is how we help liberate people from self-deception and usher them into a new and better reality.

As I think back on my time as a campus minister, there is one story that stands out when it comes to illustrating the power of questions versus statements when it comes to leading people to the truth—and it happened during one of the scariest encounters I ever had on campus.

An Unlikely Visitor

Late on a Sunday afternoon, Britany, a student from our fellowship, called me from the ministry house. The house was a simple building in the heart of campus that consisted of a large chapel-like room, a handful of offices, and a small kitchen. Britany was one of our more mature and confident students, which is why I was so surprised by the tone of her voice and the purpose of her call.

She sounded scared and said she was getting a creepy vibe because it looked as if someone had moved into the house. This was a publicly accessible building that hundreds of students routinely treated as if it were their second dorm, so I didn't understand her concern that it looked as if someone had moved in.

"Do you mean someone has ransacked the place?" I asked.

"Oh, no," she said. "It's actually cleaner than it's ever been."

My curiosity was now piqued, and within minutes, I was standing by her side, trying to unravel this mystery. At the center of every room, a lit candle had been precariously placed on a paper plate. The sun was just going down, filling the living room with an eerie glow. Britany was right—this was creepy.

In addition to the candles, someone had placed a Bible in every window sill and turned them all to face out, as if to keep away evil. As Britany and I slowly walked around, we hoped to discover that this was an elaborate joke, but it became clear that this was something other than a college prank.

We walked in silence and simply pointed to the things that stood out. The computer on the east wall was now on the west wall. The dishes from the top cabinet were now under the sink. Pictures of people had been taken down, while pictures without people remained in place. We even noticed that there were underwear soaking in the kitchen sink! What was going on?

We both felt as if we'd been dropped into a real-life horror movie. Our minds were racing, and goosebumps covered our skin. Just when we thought things couldn't get any more disturbing, we heard the squeak of the front door slowly opening. Whoever this was, we were about to meet them.

A short, disheveled-looking woman of about forty years of age boldly walked in with a large, black garbage bag slung over her shoulder. When she saw us, she abruptly stopped, cocked her head to the side, and locked her eyes with ours. Without hesitation, she dropped the bag, kept eye contact, and briskly walked right up to me. She was close enough that I could feel her breath, and I could now see the fullness of the crazy in her eyes. Before I could speak, she eerily whispered, "I've been expecting you. Come in and have a seat." She promptly turned, walked to a couch, and sat down.

I couldn't believe what was happening. Uncertain of what to say, I decided to state the obvious truth. I cleared my throat and said, as gently yet directly as I knew how, "Um . . . this is not your house."

"It most certainly is!" she shouted.

Her abrupt response caught me off guard, and I was suddenly afraid she might become violent. The only way I knew to proceed was to speak the truth again. In the most loving way, I could, I said, "Ma'am, actually, this is not your house." This, too, was met with a shout, "This is my house because I found it!"

A Calming Affect

At this point, it was obvious that she was deeply disturbed and profoundly confused. One thing was clear: I needed to get to the other room to call 911. Britany sensed that it was her job to run interference, and what she did next completely changed the dynamic for the better. She started asking questions.

"So how often do you have company?" Britany asked. The woman's demeanor immediately changed. Her shoulders dropped slightly as a wave of calm rolled over her. Britany's question seemed to sooth the woman. She took a moment to collect herself, took a deep breath, and calmly responded, "I'd say once or twice a week."

"What do you usually serve your guests?" Britany asked. The woman, now completely at peace, responded with an almost sing-song tone, "Oh, usually coffee or tea."

I was amazed at what I was seeing. Britany's questions completely changed the woman's disposition. Slowly, her answers began to bring her back to reality. By the time the police arrived, she was cool and compliant. This is an example of our human condition. You and I are not that different. We, like this woman, may too find ourselves in a season where we are not seeing the whole picture. We may not have a chemical imbalance, but we are often very confused and living out of a false reality. Let's be honest—our perception is not always accurate. When we are in this state, statements of fact—like the ones I gave the woman—are not that helpful. If you need further examples, just ask the parent of a teenager. I think we can all attest that having allegations thrown in our faces, no matter how accurate, will do little to curb our behavior. When our perception of reality is challenged, statements almost always cause us to feel cornered, and our natural response is to double down and dig in our heels. Sincere questions, however, draw us out of the corners, allowing us to look at our situation with at least some objectivity. This should make us rethink our approach as leaders, counselors, and friends. It's not always a bad thing to suspend our role as truthtellers in order to enter and understand their world by asking good questions.

Revealing a Deeper Truth

No matter how pure our intentions are, especially Godly intentions, we can't force matters of the heart. But many of us still try. Instead of asking open-ended questions to allow space for God to speak, we speak. It may be true that Christian memes, verses, and sermons hold powerful truths, but only if there is an environment of trust. It's only when people sit long enough with a god that they trust that a deeper truth is revealed. A truth that is unique to them, not regurgitated from us.

This is why it's so important that we flip the script from formal teaching to self-discovery. It's high time that we take a hard look at our culture's highly ineffective, lecture-oriented approach to learning. It's this formal teaching style that has dominated not only our universities but our churches as well.

As we develop a personal mission beyond the walls of church, we need to offer people a different experience, one that offers transformation rather than information. Transformation rarely comes from memorizing information; it comes from questioning it. Our job is to help ask those questions.

Jesus was the best at this. He asked at least 307 questions that we know of. He, no doubt, knew the answers to every question, so why did he ask? Because he was creating moments of self-discovery—a way for people to sit long enough with God that he could reveal a deeper truth. One example of this was when Jesus asked his disciples a very important question. Perhaps *the* most important question.

> When Jesus came to the region of Caesarea Philippi, he asked his disciples, "Who do people say the Son of Man is?"
>
> They replied, "Some say John the Baptist; others say Elijah; and still others, Jeremiah or one of the prophets."
>
> "But what about you?" he asked. "Who do you say I am?"
>
> Simon Peter answered, "You are the Messiah, the Son of the living God."

> Jesus replied, "Blessed are you, Simon, son of Jonah, for this was not revealed to you by flesh and blood, but by my Father in heaven." (Matthew 16:13-17 NIV)

Jesus knew that true transformation comes from accepting the deeper truth of who he is and why he came. So, he asked, "Who do you say I am?" It's not clear from the text how much time passed before Peter answered, but profoundly deep questions often take time to digest. Peter's answer pleases Jesus, not only because of the conclusion he drew but also because of how he drew it. "Blessed are you, Simon, son of Jonah, for this was not revealed to you by flesh and blood, but by my Father in heaven."

Surrendering to Jesus and his deeper ways requires more than a cognitive recognition of the truth. It requires a transformation that can only come when we slow down enough to allow God to mysteriously interact with us. It was a question that paved the way for this miracle to happen with Peter, and the same is true today.

I've noticed that most people who are far from God are not as afraid of hard questions as they are of hard statements. Chances are that you inherently understand this, so you hesitate to take offense. In fact, you may even be afraid to talk about your own relationship with Jesus because you don't want to be perceived as harsh or judgmental. If so, then the solution is simple—ask questions and let God work while you remain silent. If we want God to enter the equation in the same way he did with Peter, we need to give him space to work. It's amazing what a question and attentive listening can do. If you can discipline yourself to ask sincere questions without feeling the need to immediately answer them, I believe you will experience results in ways that formal teaching or confronting someone with the truth could never provide.

A Practical Pathway

To ask questions that have the power to reveal deeper truths, we first need to establish trust. So how do we do that? I love the approach taken by a business owner in Waco, Texas, named Chris DeLeenheer. He has a passion to make everyone in his life a priority, not a project. To be intentional about building increasing levels of trust in his relationships, he came up with four categories of questions that move progressively from surface issues to heart issues:

- Casual questions
- Meaningful questions
- Spiritual questions
- Discovery questions

Casual questions may seem obvious, but just because the topic is rooted in the familiarity of sports or Netflix doesn't mean it isn't significant. Even casual questions can lead to a deeper relationship. The purpose of asking casual questions isn't about making chit-chat around casual topics; it's about asking questions. If you find that the relationships in your life feel stagnant, it might be related to how much you're talking rather than listening.

Meaningful questions often revolve around family and health. It's a good way to take the next step into a deeper relationship. The manner in which we respect the answers we hear will go a long way toward developing credibility. If you sense a hesitancy at any point along this process, take a break. Eye contact, head nods, and other forms of active listening are all ways of demonstrating that we're listening, which is essential for developing trust. Do not underestimate how quickly a significant bond can develop. I know too many Christians who assume that this process of building trust is always years in the making. That may be true in some cases, but only if we never intentionally move to a deeper set of questions.

Spiritual questions are easier to ask than you may think. Simply asking what someone's religious background is will often open up a spiritual conversation in a way that feels comfortable rather than awkward. Don't assume people do not want to be asked spiritual questions. Our culture has made the topic of religion and spirituality taboo. However, asking people about their experiences is rarely taboo. I've noticed that even the most unspiritual people may be quick to talk about their experiences or perceptions of religion and spirituality. You may be surprised at who is willing to have a conversation about spiritual topics, especially if you're intentional about building trust.

Discovery questions require the deepest level of trust. Discovery questions are different than spiritual questions in that they are questions that connect to what the Bible has to say. Consequently, it is these discovery-based questions that make room for the Spirit of God to participate. It's this common ground of self-discovery that welcomes all people to contribute. The most effective tool I know for revealing a deeper truth is a Discovery Bible Study. It's a question-based Bible study that has proven to be the leading tool in gospel movements worldwide.

Chris' conviction is to not move on to the next category of questions until that person is comfortable within that category. For example, if he senses that a person is hesitant to talk about their home life, Chris will keep his questions casual for a while. It's this respectful approach that quickly develops trust. As I've adopted this approach, I've noticed how quickly some people move through this process. Sometimes all in the same conversation. What I've concluded is that asking these questions is a highly practical way to determine who my "people of peace" are. People who are willing to join me at the pinnacle of meaningful self-discovery. A place where God is invited into the conversation.

Discovery Bible Study

Discovery Bible Study (DBS) is a brilliant, question-based technique designed to welcome non-Christians into a judgment-free zone with the Bible. The secret is using questions rather than statements to lead the study. What makes this especially appealing to someone who is unfamiliar with the Bible is that it requires zero preparation. All that is required is to read a section of Scripture and ask the same four questions every time.

- What did I learn about God?
- What did I learn about people?
- What do I feel compelled to do?
- Who else needs to hear this message?

I introduced the DBS model to my good friend Mark, who is a missionary in Thailand. Mark was experiencing ministry fatigue. He was constantly hosting events and preparing lessons. Within a few months of implementing this question-based approach to study, he was astonished at both the results it produced and how little preparation it required. He described it as effortlessly effective.

Because DBS is intended for those who are not yet Christians, I've found that it's us established Christians who have the hardest time with this discovery method. We have been trained to teach lessons, quote books, and refer to sermons. Consequently, the DBS format doesn't work well in Christian circles because, quite frankly, Christians get in the way. But if we are serious about developing a personal mission outside of those circles, this is a tool worth using.

Keith is another good friend who started using the DBS method in Honduras. He is one of the few people I know who had the courage to alter his ministry approach of twenty-plus years to something that appeared to be the opposite of everything he had previously believed to be true. Like many of us, he believed that the only way people would understand and receive the good news was through direct statements. His approach was to preach *at* people, either through public gatherings or door-to-door. He didn't love that he was perceived as pushy and obnoxious, but it was his concern for people that compelled him to keep trying.

As you may have guessed, his approach produced little to no fruit. In three years, he had three people surrender to Jesus. It was not the success he was hoping for. Instead of hiding behind statements like, "Well, I guess this is God's will," or "My job is just to be faithful," he had the courage to change. He began using a DBS approach, and although the results were slow at first, he and his team experimented and eventually stumbled on a unique opportunity. They noticed that many of the people they were reaching out to were illiterate. Obviously, this made studying the Bible a huge challenge. What they did next was revolutionary. They began to record the text and the questions on a tape recorder. This made the groups even more leaderless. It didn't take long for it to feel like the recorder was leading the meeting. Consequently, it empowered a much wider group of people to initiate more meetings. Before long, people were asking if they could take the recorder home to their families or to work. It was amazing to see how so many people, even people who didn't consider themselves Christians, wanted to share this recorder full of life.

All types of people were encouraged to participate. Some were trained, but many were not. It triggered a movement of God that was impossible to control or contain. Within the next ten years, Keith saw over 25,000 people surrender to Jesus. He smiles as he tells me that story. "It's so much easier and more fruitful when we let God do the work," he says. Indeed, questions are more powerful than statements.

So, what do we learn from this? How do we let God do the work in our own contexts? Although the answers may not always be obvious, I do believe our best way forward is tied to asking questions that promote self-discovery.

So, what's stopping you? Are you willing to be among the brave few who take the risk of experimenting? Questions are something you can implement right now. If you want a personal mission that is known for transformation rather than information, it's time to flip the script from formal teaching to self-discovery.

PART 3 PERMISSION TO FLIP THE SCRIPT: DEVELOPING A NEW SEQUENCE OF ORDER

9. TIME BEFORE INVITATION

There is an assumption among many Christians in the West that the primary way to see godly transformation in the lives of our friends and family is to somehow get them to church. I question how effective one hour on a Sunday morning has ever been, but in today's culture, just getting people to attend for that hour has never been harder. With more and more church scandals being reported, the trustworthiness of the established church has reached a new low. In addition, the convenience of our online world has produced a growing number of people who don't want to go anywhere, including the store. Could it be that before the invitation is offered, there is another investment that we should implement? An investment modeled by Jesus himself? I'm speaking of the investment of time.

There are two questions I love to ask people who work in paid ministry. The first is, "How did you get into ministry?" Without exception, the answer to this question is always tied to a respected person who invested time in their life. The second question is, "What are you currently most excited about in your ministry?" The answer almost always has to do with a church program. I think that's because ministry leaders are always thinking about reaching the masses. But the success of virtually all outreach programs always comes down to who you ride with to the event or who you eat with afterward. In other words, it's the kneecap-to-kneecap relationships that make the difference. Ministry programs aren't bad, as long as we remember that their point is to help people mingle with the right people. In fact, even the most mediocre of programs can have a great impact if there are quality people dispersed throughout the group. That's because making a relational investment almost always yields a return.

As you develop your personal mission, it is imperative that you flip the script by focusing on who we invest our time with. Time, as it turns out, has benefits that invitation can never provide.

The Trajectory Principle

Show me your friends, and I'll show you your future. That's the trajectory principle. If there is one truth that has shaped me and my ministry philosophy more than anything else, it is this: *You become who you spend time with.* That's why I am immensely grateful for the friends I had in college. Up to that point, I was surrounded by people who certainly were not challenging me for the better. I loved my high school friends, but none of us could see past the next party. We weren't mature enough to understand that a self-absorbed lifestyle wouldn't stand the test of time.

To hide my partying ways, I developed the habit of lying to my parents. In fact, I lied my way out of so many situations that I began to believe I was invincible. So, when I discovered that my family was going away for a week, I considered this a gift that was almost too good to be true. It was my chance to throw a party of my own—in a house full of antiques and breakables. What could possibly go wrong? I was smart enough to move all the delicate items into a closed-off bedroom but too stupid to first photograph the contents of each room. When the party was over and it was time to put everything back in its rightful place, I panicked. Every knickknack looked the same to me. Suddenly, I didn't even know which pictures to hang on the wall. Decorative plates from above the fireplace were now in the China cabinet. It was awful.

Upon my parents' return, it took all of two seconds for my mother to notice everything. And when I say everything, I mean that she now saw through all of my many lies. The disappointment in her face forced me to look at my life in a way I never had before. As I sat in the backyard and stared at our house, I realized I was on a bad trajectory, one that would require continuing to live a life of cover-ups and lies. It was my first glimpse of who I was becoming, and I didn't like what I saw. If I was going to change my trajectory, I needed to spend time with new people.

Two New Friends

Following graduation, I enrolled in Bible college and met Brad and Sam, two friends who radically changed the track I was on and whose influence I carry with me to this day. Three decades later, we are all still in ministry and all still benefiting from the lessons we learned while sharing dorm life together.

Even though we were students at a Bible college, none of us were particularly spiritual or theological. But one thing we all innately understood was the power of investing time with one another. We were with each other all day in classes, and then we hung out all evening together in the dorm. We didn't have much in the way of material resources, but we did have an abundance of the most valuable commodity—time.

These new friends were not the partiers I was used to hanging out with, but we did have fun. We were always coming up with new ways to entertain ourselves. This usually involved some sort of ball and a random piece of furniture. We may have broken a few lamps, but we also had community in spades. In addition to fun and games, we were also committed to bettering one another. We gave ourselves permission to speak truth into one another's lives. As young guys, it was inevitable that at least one of us would say something stupid or act in an inappropriate manner. Over time, we got better at calling each other out and even initiating positive challenges in one another. It was during these college years that I learned to prioritize relationships over accomplishments.

Brad had a heart for international students, especially those from China. He spent numerous hours with these students at Michigan State University's campus across town. He was always learning new Chinese phrases and trying new foods while simultaneously providing these students with used furniture and driving lessons. MSU is where Brad still ministers today. The fruit of Brad's ministry has never been wide, but it's always been deep. If you were to visit Brad's campus ministry today, you probably wouldn't find a packed assembly for a worship service. But if you were to meet with Brad's alumni, you'd see how many of his characteristics have shaped their lives. This is what discipleship looks like.

Sam's time investment wasn't as targeted. His ministry mantra was and is, "Ministry is never bigger than the person in front of you." Sam's simple obedience to loving the person in front of him has made him the most available person I know. If I were to call Sam right now, I know he would answer the phone. If he's at the grocery store or about to sit down for dinner, he'll just bring me along on his ear. While I understand and acknowledge the need to protect one's time, I also can't help but appreciate the gift of availability. Jesus did both. He protected his time by getting away for prayer and rest with his disciples, but he was also interruptible. In fact, it's a challenge to find a significant interaction with Jesus in which he wasn't interrupted. I can't tell you how many times I've seen God use Sam in mighty ways simply because he was willing to interrupt what he was doing to give someone a ride, talk to a stranger, or change someone's oil on the spot. And his willingness to prioritize relationships through constant availability has led him to some of the most obscure yet fruitful mission fields.

What I learned from these two friends is that leveraging my time to make a relational investment in others will always be our greatest ministry resource. There is no substitute. Knowing how simple and effective that initial ministry season was has spoiled me. It's created an obsession within me to find new ways in today's culture to replicate more disciples like the ones that were made back in that dorm. How and with whom we spend our time will dictate our interests, our values, and our perspective. Again, show me your friends, and I'll show you your future.

The Discipleship Genius of Jesus

Jesus shared life with lots of people, but he made an intentional time investment in the Twelve. It's believed that he had well over a hundred followers at the time he selected the Twelve. Here is one of the most unassuming yet profound texts that gives us insight into that process.

> Jesus went up on a mountainside and called to him those he wanted, and they came to him. He appointed twelve that they might be with him. (Mark 3:13-15)

It appears that Jesus' plan to change the world was to pick people he wanted to be with and who wanted to be with him. The text also provides Jesus' strategy, "that they might be with him." It sounds pretty unassuming, but it makes perfect sense to those of us who have been deeply impacted by the people with whom we spend our time.

Information is consumed, but time is experienced. One of the great falsehoods we have embraced in the Western world is that the consumption of information is king. Somewhere along the way, we have concluded that knowledge equals understanding. But knowledge does not equal understanding. For example, knowing how a bicycle works doesn't mean you understand how to ride one. And a similar principle applies to discipleship. In fact, I recently attended an incredible Sunday school class on discipling as Jesus did. There is nothing I would have added or subtracted to make the presentation better. Yet, I'm fairly certain that no one from that class began discipling others because of it.

Compare that approach to that of my friend Cody. Cody is an alumnus of mine who runs a community care center in a small town. He has a desire to make disciples of Jesus while meeting the practical needs of those in his community who struggle with poverty and a lack of education. His mission is clear: neighbors help neighbors reach their full potential. This is an empowerment ministry. Not a handout ministry. Watching ministry recipients turn around and become ministry contributors is what this ministry is all about. How does this work? The answer is simpler than you might think. Like Jesus, their approach is to place good, godly, and healthy people in proximity to neighbors who need help. How does he train these initial healthy people? Well, I can tell you that it doesn't involve spending time in a classroom. Instead, in the same way that Jesus did, he handpicks people he *wants to be with*, then models it in front of the neighbors. Even the training sessions held in private look more like a role-playing exercise. These trained ministry partners may not always be able to explain their role with words, but they sure can show you with their actions. It's this on-going modeling that is eventually picked up and applied by those being ministered to. The result is that discipleship is multiplied.

Spending intentional time with others has always been and will always be the most powerful tool in God's kingdom. That's the discipleship genius of Jesus. And while it might be hard to find examples of those who live it out in our busy world, there is no shortage of examples in the wider world. A world that's slow enough to prioritize relationships.

Three Mile an Hour God

There is a common saying within disciple-making movements worldwide: *You have to go slow in order to go fast.* The idea is that a long-term investment in people produces stable and long-lasting disciples who will continue making disciples for a lifetime. Here in the United States, however, we have an appetite for instant results. Which means we are less concerned with developing people and more concerned with delivering a message. There is very little in our culture that honors or encourages the slower pace of a long-term investment.

One of the voices challenging this mindset is a Japanese theologian named Kosuke Koyama. Kosuke has traveled extensively worldwide, and his analysis is that a slower pace of life matches God's pace of life. He makes the argument that God moves at three miles per hour, which is the average speed of two people walking together. He believes so strongly in the potential gospel impact of this slower pace that he wrote a book called *Three Mile an Hour God*. In Chapter 7, we considered how prayer walks are a tangible way for us to align ourselves with what God cares about, and I believe there is a similar principle at work when it comes to discipleship—that choosing a slow and steady approach to investing in others is how we align ourselves with Jesus' model of discipleship.

Having spent time in multiple developing countries, I can testify that life indeed moves much, much slower there. Whether I was in Liberia, the Philippines, or Kenya, life looked relatively similar. Communities were small, and resources were few, but so were the distractions. People walked everywhere, so everything took more time. Even trips to the store felt less like an errand and more like an event. And what do people do when they walk? They talk. As I look back on my experiences on the mission field, I can now see that many of the significant moments happened when I was walking with my friends at roughly three miles per hour.

Could it be that flipping the script from invitation to time is just as possible in our fast-paced culture? Could it also be that herein lies the secret to the greatest benefit of all? Discipleship.

Lifestyle Discipleship

My wife, Paulette, is not a churchy woman. She has never sung in the choir, played the piano, taught a Sunday school class, or headed up a vacation Bible school program. But she is one of the best disciple-makers I know, and her method may surprise you.

Paulette has a reputation as a selfless person who is always finding ways to leverage her life for others. She's been known to gather furniture for immigrant families from Congo, make numerous visits to comfort friends in the hospital, volunteer at school functions, and leave a $50 tip for a sick girl working the drive-through. But those aren't the primary beneficiaries of her discipling efforts. The ones she was really discipling were our kids, who were sitting in the back seat of the car or tagging along while she did those things. I've come to understand that what we model with our lives is the most effective and Jesus-like form of discipleship.

My college friends and I didn't know it at the time, but we were discipling one another in the way we lived our lives and prioritized our relationships. It's not all that different from what I hear from others who have been the benefactors of such life-transforming discipleship. They often say, "I didn't even know I was being discipled!"

There's a good chance that the most profound effect of your personal mission may have less to do with what you accomplish and more to do with whom you choose to accomplish it with. Your effectiveness for the kingdom does not depend on your ability to reach all of your goals, to juggle lots of things, or to run harder and faster. Instead, it will depend on your willingness to pull the right people close as you walk in step with Jesus at three miles per hour.

10. AUTHORITY BEFORE ASSIGNMENT

An Unlikely Mentor

Al Hamilton, God rest his soul, was by far the most eccentric person I've ever known. Tall and slender with exaggerated facial features, he reminded me of a cartoon character. His eyebrows were big and bushy, and he moved his arms incessantly. He often talked to himself in a falsetto voice, carrying on complete conversations using quotes from *The Little Mermaid* or old *Pink Panther* movies. And he laughed almost as much as he breathed. He didn't really seem to care what people thought of him, which made it easy for him to say what he was thinking, even if it meant talking to himself. At best, he gave off the appearance of silliness; at worst, he may have appeared to be insane. However, looking back, I can see that for all of his eccentricities, Al was what you might call crazy like a fox. When it came to challenging people to go on the mission field, Al was as intentional and clever as they come.

I first met Al at a campus ministry retreat when I was in college. He was unlike any speaker I had ever heard. His delivery was harsh; his cadence was sporadic, but his message was clear: *Go!* On the surface, Al was a man in his late fifties who was the founder and director of a mission's organization. However, I think Al's primary work was to disrupt the status quo. When he was occasionally invited to speak at Bible colleges, he wouldn't be invited back. He'd inevitably blurt out something like, "Drop out of school and go live your adventure." You can see why he didn't gain a lot of support from the establishment. However, as college kids, we loved him! In fact, it was his words that convinced me to give up a year of schooling to live as a missionary in Hungary. It was his quote that still rings in my ears to this day, "If you ask the president of the United States for a gift, you don't ask for something that your parents could provide. And when you go to God, ask for God-sized gifts. Don't ask for a car. Ask for a country!"

It was Al who helped me realize that kingdom work had little to do with my credentials. It was *availability,* not *ability,* that Jesus was looking for. Al was full of one-liners that not only made me stop and think but also made me take a leap of faith. I can still remember him saying, "It is impossible to stand on God's promises while sitting on the premises." He was convinced that a life of godliness equated to a life of action. It was Al's challenges that pushed me to start campus ministries in three countries by the age of twenty-six.

Al was a walking catalyst for missions, and anyone in his path was fair game. No one was safe. Christians or non-Christians. Trained or untrained. Young or old. He felt that everyone should *go.* He told me stories of atheists coming to faith because he convinced them to build a house in Mexico. Al's passion to ignite movements wasn't without controversy. On one occasion, he was sought out by someone struggling with suicidal thoughts. His response? "If you are set on dying, then I would suggest you smuggle some Bibles. I know of three countries where you will get shot for sure." His approach was unorthodox and extreme, but coming from a world where everything was predictable and orderly, I found his strategy refreshing.

Ready or Not

There is one consistent fear that seems to be shared by anyone who has dared to consider acting on the authority of Jesus: *I'm not ready.* It's easy to convince ourselves that we have more to learn before we can put ourselves out there. But since there will always be more to learn, this creates a never-ending cycle that keeps many of us from ever taking action. I think somewhere down deep, we believe that ministers are the only ones who have learned enough. It's the minister who possesses qualifications—special training, unique gifts, or an earned degree—that we do not have, and so we disqualify ourselves before we even start. And yet, we need to remember that Jesus consistently released people before they thought they were ready.

Do you remember the story about how Jesus healed a man from a legion of demons? The man was cutting himself and naked one minute and in his right mind the next after an encounter with Jesus. If ever there were a time when it might have seemed prudent to test the authenticity of someone's conversion and readiness before sending them out for a mission, this would seem to have been a textbook case. If it had been up to me, I definitely would have waited a month or two to make sure his conversion was legit. It just makes sense, doesn't it? Shouldn't people need to prove themselves by successfully completing a few assignments before we give them authority? Assignment before authority seems to be the correct order. But that wasn't Jesus' way. He flipped the script.

> As Jesus was getting into the boat, the man who had been demon-possessed begged to go with him. Jesus did not let him, but said, "Go home to your own people and tell them how much the Lord has done for you, and how he has had mercy on you." So, the man went away and began to tell in the Decapolis how much Jesus had done for him. And all the people were amazed. (Mark 5:18–20 NIV)

Did you catch that? Jesus turned down the request of a new believer to follow him because he wanted him to go preach. On what grounds was the demon-possessed man qualified? Was he properly trained? Was he given assignments to prove he was trustworthy? Nope. On the same day he was healed, Jesus released him to do ministry on his own. And it wasn't the only time Jesus did this. Remember the outcast woman at the well in Samaria? She, too, proclaimed the good news on the same day Jesus taught her about living water. The principle in both stories is the same: after you've encountered Jesus, you have instant authority to share how his good news has affected you. This is the same for us. Once good news enters our lives, we immediately get to share that good news. And like the demon-possessed man, bystanders will look on with amazement.

I can still remember being picked up by Al on a Sunday morning. We were going to visit one of his supporting churches about two hours away. It was about ten minutes into our trip when he told me that I would be preaching that morning. When I let him know that I had never preached before and didn't feel ready, he said, "That's okay. Most people sleep anyway."

So, for the remainder of that two-hour drive, I fought through self-doubt as I wove together a hodgepodge of thoughts connected to random bits of Scripture. By the time we arrived, Al had helped convince me that what I had was a divine revelation. In actuality, it was rough. The content was probably acceptable, but I was nervous. It was scary enough to visit a church for the first time, let alone preach my first sermon off of chicken scratches written in the moving car. I don't remember much about the sermon itself, other than stumbling through it like a novice. But I do remember the overwhelmingly positive response from the congregants. Although they knew it was my first time preaching and had the grace to overlook the imperfections, what we all experienced that morning was nothing less than divine. I simply spoke from the heart. I didn't have time to learn any other way. The results were powerful. The congregation was filled with something more than empathy and compassion for some kid who was put on the spot. It was almost as if they were amazed! There is something that moves within our soul, is there not, when we witness a pure attempt from the unrefined. But the experience of the congregants paled in comparison to the feeling I had as the unrefined messenger. No longer did I see myself as the insignificant kid who jumped in the car that morning. I now saw myself as Al saw me and as God saw me. I was now God's ambassador. Words can't express the gratitude I felt then and continue to feel now. All because Al took a chance on a kid who *wasn't ready*.

So how about you? Do you feel ready? Or do you feel paralyzed by the thought of making a mistake or doing something wrong?

Just Do Something

I met my friend Mandi when I had the privilege of serving as an interim pastor at the church she attended. Although she was a follower of Jesus and served as an administrative assistant at the church, the thought that she might be on the front lines for Jesus was initially a completely foreign idea. It was only through the authority she found in Jesus that she came out of her shell and started living out her personal mission within her small town. It was her inexperience that ended up being her greatest asset. It was almost as if she didn't know better. She took my suggestions to heart, and before I knew it, she was boldly asking people from her gym to go on prayer walks and to start Discovery Bible Studies. Her husband, who had also never been in ministry, picked up on her example. He started doing something that felt small and inconsequential, but it was at least something. He began asking spiritual questions with his workmates and started a weekly DBS with his extended family. These seemingly insignificant steps of obedience were noticed by others, and he is now serving as the head elder at his local church.

Never did Mandi imagine that her willingness to live out her mission would ultimately affect so many people around her, and ultimately lead her to work for a mission organization where her role is to empower other people to also act on what God has prompted them to do. By way of motivation, she often uses a quote from the movie *The Nutty Professor*: "Just do something! Just do something!" For those like Brett and Mandi who dare to just do something, there is often a sweet reward. But for many of us, we need a bit more structure before we jump. We need to be trained.

A Training Session with Jesus

Wouldn't it be nice if everything we would need to carry out our personal mission was clearly spelled out for us by Jesus himself? What a gift that would be. Oh, wait! Jesus *did* lead a training session. In fact, he actually led two training sessions! One in Mathew 10 and the other in Luke 10; one for the Twelve and the other for the seventy-two. Both trainings are strikingly similar, and both embody an approach that applies the five flipped scripts we have just covered.

Session 1

> Jesus called his twelve disciples to him and gave them authority to drive out impure spirits and to heal every disease and sickness.
>
> These are the names of the twelve apostles: first, Simon (who is called Peter) and his brother Andrew; James son of Zebedee and his brother John; Philip and Bartholomew; Thomas and Matthew the tax collector; James son of Alphaeus and Thaddaeus; Simon the Zealot and Judas Iscariot, who betrayed him.
>
> These twelve Jesus sent out with the following instructions: "Do not go among the Gentiles or enter any town of the Samaritans. Go rather to the lost sheep of Israel. As you go, proclaim this message: 'The kingdom of heaven has come near.' Heal the sick, raise the dead, cleanse those who have leprosy, and drive out demons. Freely you have received; freely give.
>
> "Do not get any gold or silver or copper to take with you in your belts—no bag for the journey or extra shirt or sandals or a staff, for the worker is worth his keep. Whatever town or village you enter, search there for some worthy person and stay at their house until you leave." (Matthew 10:1–11 NIV)

Session 2

> After this the Lord appointed seventy-two others and sent them two by two ahead of him to every town and place where he was about to go. He told them, "The harvest is plentiful, but the workers are few. Ask the Lord of the harvest, therefore, to send out workers into his harvest field. Go! I am sending you out like lambs among wolves. Do not take a purse or bag or sandals; and do not greet anyone on the road."
>
> "When you enter a house, first say, 'Peace to this house.' If someone who promotes peace is there, your peace will rest on them; if not, it will return to you. Stay there, eating and drinking whatever they give you, for the worker deserves his wages. Do not move around from house to house.
>
> "When you enter a town and are welcomed, eat what is offered to you. Heal the sick who are there and tell them, 'The kingdom of God has come near to you.'" (Luke 10:1-9 NIV)

Did you recognize how Jesus flipped the scripts?

Being before doing. Jesus said, "Freely you have received; freely give." You can't share what you don't have.

Chaos before order. Jesus sent them out as lambs among wolves.

Self-discovery before formal teaching. The only message He tells them to share is that the kingdom of heaven is near. This appears to be an experiential message rather than an instructional one.

Time before invitation. Jesus tells his disciples to 'Stay there, eating and drinking whatever they give you. Do not move around from house to house.'

Authority before assignment. Finally, it is Jesus' emphasis on authority before assignment that stands out most. Never before had the disciples cast out demons or healed the sick. It was only when they boldly brought peace to a new territory that they saw the manifestation of Jesus' authority. Could it be that the reason most of us have never experienced a manifestation of Jesus' authority in our lives is because we fail to take that authority to new places? Consistent with his training of the disciples, Jesus starts his Great Commission—to them and to us—with the same offer of his authority.

> Then Jesus came to them and said, "All authority in heaven and on earth has been given to me. Therefore, go and make disciples of all nations." (Matthew 28:18-19 NIV)

What a statement! *All* authority in heaven and on earth is his. Every last bit of it. Without his authority, we have nothing but a really great plan. We're like well-designed race cars with no fuel. But with his authority, we have everything. We have the strength to carry out our personal mission. Although Jesus doesn't spell out the details about how we are to make disciples, he clearly gives us his authority to go anywhere and everywhere. For those who dare to try something, Jesus promises, "And surely I am with you always, to the very end of the age" (Matthew 28:20 niv).

Not until recent years have I noticed that this verse seems to be a promise to those who obey Jesus' Great Commission. It's this idea that explains the disproportional amount of grace that seems to have followed me all my life. I don't consider myself to be very disciplined in my pursuit of intimacy with God. My prayer time is inconsistent, my scripture reading is sparse, and my journaling is nonexistent. Yet, I would say that I feel like I've received an unreasonable amount of God's blessing and presence that can be explained only because of my obedience to his commission. This seems to be true for my colleagues as well.

My friend Rick is the campus minister at Georgia Tech. Rick will be the first to admit he isn't as smart as his bright engineering students. His Bible knowledge is basic, and he also has little to no interest in theology. He simply loves Jesus and his students more than many of them love themselves. And one thing he does better than anyone else is release people. Rick has sent more students to the mission field than any campus minister I've ever met. His gift of convincing chemical engineering graduates to give up triple-digit salaries so they can live as poor missionaries has produced campus ministries throughout Europe, Thailand, Mexico, and Australia.

In summary, there is an extraordinary amount of freedom, fruit, and fun that Jesus offers those who are willing to simply go. Like eighth-grade kids roaming the amusement park of life, we get to see his kingdom unfold before us. It would serve us well to suspend our self-doubts and fears long enough to listen to the voices of people such as Rick and Al, both of whom leveraged their unorthodox lives to convince those in earshot to just do something. Remember, most of the students who heeded their words had no idea what they were doing when they were sent, but they all seemed to figure it out. I guess that's the way it's supposed to be in kingdom work. We learn as we go. We trust as we go. We grow as we go. Maybe what we are missing most today isn't better preparation. Maybe we just need to heed the call of the crazy people who preach that one resilient message: *Go!*

PART 4

PERMISSION TO START FIRES: DEVELOPING CONTAGIOUS ASPIRATION

Freedom is never more than one generation away from extinction.
—Ronald Regan

If you want your personal mission to make an ongoing impact, it will need to engage other people. The fruition of every Jesus-centered mission should be to multiply a personal mission in others. If we aren't intentional about fostering fresh dreams in those around us, then we are not contributing to a movement. We are building an empire. Something owned and controlled by one group. In this sense, empires don't have to be big in order to squelch organic growth; they only have to be self-contained. If your only experience with the church is that of an empire, it will be important for you in this section to do your best to suspend that mental image, allowing a new and possibly foreign idea to take its place. Fortunately, current trends are moving us as a culture away from centralized empires toward a culture that is more decentralized. It's refreshing to see the number of churches, even traditional ones, that no longer see themselves as holding tanks, but more as launching pads. As the big empire churches that were built in the 1990s begin to shift and, in some cases, crumble, we can't make the mistake of replacing them with little empires. Each missional entity that we birth ultimately needs to become a launching pad of *its* own. Whether it's a care center, an after-school program, or your workplace, these settings for personal mission must provide the gift that keeps on giving—permission. When your personal mission is working best, it will draw in a whole new sector of unchurched people; allowing them to catch an idea of their own. Could it be that this is what ecclesia (the gathering of the outward) was intended to be? A plethora of "churches" scattered throughout town, all as diverse as the callings of the people within them? Doesn't it seem that Jesus intended the church to be a series of kinetic reactions, spreading itself everywhere? If so, then perhaps church planting should look less like an affluently placed country club and more like a movement of spiritual fire starters.

There is nothing in our world quite like fire. It's hot magic that has a way of mesmerizing us all. In addition to its alluring nature, fire has always been a fundamental component of sustaining life. For most of human history, it was pretty simple: without fire, you died. Hence, there was a time when everyone learned how to build fires. Today, fire is looked at much differently. In our controlled environments, we no longer see fire as a predominant source of our existence. It's now seen as something dangerous, and fire building is reserved for the few.

In that sense, we've become domesticated—we no longer know how to build and sustain fires. And a similar principle is true when it comes to building and sustaining *spiritual* fires. We're living at a time when so many of us have been tamed by our experience of life within the walls of the church that we no longer know how to build spiritual fires beyond them. Why would we? One of the side effects of living in a developmentally advanced society is failing to see how anything religious or otherwise could exist outside the predictability of static institutionalism. It's difficult for us in Western cultures to envision a scenario in which we initiate something new without it being attached to a corporation or an LLC. The church, however, was never meant to be contained or institutionalized. It is supposed to move fluidly throughout our city. If we want to see the positive impact of a spiritual brushfire sweeping our community, we need to know how to start spiritual fires—and that requires knowing how they work.

PART 4 PERMISSION TO START FIRES: DEVELOPING CONTAGIOUS ASPIRATION

11. FIRE REQUIRES FRICTION

I like to think of myself as a guy who can rough it. There was a time in my youth when I didn't think twice about traveling to remote parts of the upper peninsula in Michigan with my brother and a few buddies. I know I have it within me to live off the land, but the truth is that I just don't want to. Those adventurous outdoor weekends are now replaced by me watching *Survivor* from the comfort of my living room. When it comes to starting a fire from scratch, I know that fire requires friction. I've seen plenty of examples on one of my many screens. But do you think I've ever tried starting my own fire from scratch? Not even once. All I've ever done is sit comfortably on my couch at room temperature, cheering on those few who are voraciously rubbing sticks together. There is a big difference between my understanding that fire needs friction and actually starting a fire of my own. As confident as I am that I could learn to do it, I've yet to put myself in a situation to try.

The principles we are about to unfold regarding spiritual fire-starting will likely make quick cognitive sense. However, if you don't put yourself in a situation to try, you will remain a spectator, evaluating the church from a comfortable distance. Spiritual fire starting isn't as hard as you may think, but it does require you to get outside.

Chaos and Order

If we want to see contagious aspiration make its way throughout our city, getting outside is a must. It's only there that we will understand firsthand the necessary friction it will take to start these fires. Life outside the walls of church is unpredictable and a little uncomfortable, but once outside, God seems to take over. It's as if he is honoring those who are willing to try. I think you will find that the friction that is necessary to build a spiritual fire outside the walls of church will pale in comparison to the friction you must embrace *before* you go outside. It's causing friction *within* the church. This will be true, even if your "church" is a small missional outpost. There is just something about an established spiritual entity, no matter how small, that will always tempt us to stay inside.

Perhaps you've heard about the idea of "managing tensions," of allowing two seemingly incompatible things to coexist. That's the kind of tension or friction we need to seek out when we want to start spiritual fires. Specifically, we need to be comfortable managing the tension between chaos and order. Both dynamics need to be active if we are going to see a more mobile and decentralized version of the church. Unfortunately, many of us view this tension between order and chaos as a threat rather than a gift. And yet, if we want to ignite spiritual fires, we have to recognize that both dynamics are required. We need to accept that there are two forces that sustain a healthy church: the force that harnesses the power of order and the force that harnesses the power of chaos. Most of us intuitively understand the order side of church but are unaware of the chaos side. I certainly was unaware and would have stayed that way if not for the unique overseas opportunities that eventually opened my eyes.

Fresh Eyes in Hungary

At the start of my personal mission, I was a twenty-year-old kid who was filled with both ignorance and optimism—a dangerous combination in many people's eyes. There were more than a few people who pulled me aside and asked some challenging questions: *Under what authority are you going? How old are you? Do you even have a degree?* The truth was that I was woefully unqualified, but like the disciples, I trusted that God could do a lot with my ignorance and optimism.

I was one of seven college students who responded to an invitation to give one year to serving Jesus in another country. We put our college educations on pause to take full advantage of our single, no kids, no mortgage mobility. In the fall of 1990, we packed our bags and became exchange students in Hungary. Again, we had no formal training or Bible education. Heck, I don't think we really even had a plan. We just went on faith and trusted that Jesus would give us what we needed along the way. Looking back, I can understand the reservations some had about our trip. However, I can tell you that it was this on-the-job training that did more to prepare me for a life of ministry than all my Bible courses combined.

In Hungary, we were forced to create opportunities to advance the kingdom. There was no church service to invite people to; it was just us. So, we took a look around and asked ourselves how we could leverage our circumstances into opportunities. It was a fun and energizing season. Our primary assets were the Hungarian language partners who were assigned to us by the school. These students were advanced English speakers, and we quickly developed friendships with them. We needed help with our basic Hungarian, and they needed help with their advanced English. The Hungarians suggested that we teach them English-language songs and read to them from a book that had complicated sentence structures. Hmm, it seemed like we could come up with something like that!

Our meetings were messy—a hodgepodge of storytelling, advanced reading, and singing that naturally developed into a makeshift Bible study over time. It was this messy and, yes, chaotic approach that helped me see for the first time how church didn't have to happen at a certain time, with a certain schedule, or in a specific building. All we knew was that our new friends were asking spiritual questions, inviting their friends to join us, and even getting baptized. Even with the overwhelming amount of evidence before me, I still couldn't fully allow myself to see this beautiful expression of the kingdom of heaven as a church. However, I was taking baby steps as I analyzed this phenomenon that was unfolding before me.

In my immaturity, I made some rash conclusions. Instead of recognizing that it was an environment of chaos that was producing fruit, I was programmed to only see the order. I made the mistake of exchanging old, hard-and-fast rules for new, hard-and-fast rules. For example, I equated our early success with exchanging pews for chairs and rows for circles. I also became fixated on the importance of snacks *before* the meeting instead of after, which was how it had been in the church I'd grown up in. It seems kind of ridiculous now, right? But I had been so conditioned to adhere to the order side of church that I simply swapped one kind of rigid adherence to order for another. I had always scoffed at the stories of church splits over trivial things like the color of the carpet, but in a way, this was exactly the kind of person I was.

This might be a good place to pause for a moment so you can reflect on how you might have made something essential that isn't really essential when it comes to the things of God. For example, is there a particular denomination you consider the best or the only right way? Do you think church really counts if it doesn't happen in a church building on a Sunday? Is there a particular order of events that is essential? What if the church is led by a woman or an unpaid clergy member? Is there any kind of order you're unwilling to let go of, especially as it relates to your personal mission?

The reality is that most, if not all, of us have been trained to see church in a particular and predictable way. My point isn't to debate which details are important. I just want to help you see that we are all predisposed to a particular order in church, and sometimes we prioritize order over everything else. But remember, order is only half of the equation. If we want to start spiritual fires, we must embrace the fact that there is also a messy or chaotic side to church—a side that has been well hidden in the United States. A side that may have remained hidden from me if it hadn't been for what happened next.

A Different Yet Similar Church in China

The university we attended in Hungary had a winter break that lasted from mid-December through the end of January. While most exchange students were planning their European tours, three of us—Sonja (our team leader), Paulette (my future wife), and I—wanted to visit our friends from back home who were living out their personal missions in China. So, we booked train tickets on the Siberian Express from Budapest to Beijing for only $104 round trip! That's an eighteen-day journey—nine days each way. What I experienced on this journey had a profound effect on my life.

Beijing had an entirely different vibe than Hungary. Hungary was just emerging from Communist rule, and we felt comfortable speaking openly about spiritual things. Not so in China. The horrors of the Tiananmen Square Massacre were only months old; it was clear that any message that competed with the government would be harshly put down. Everything done in the name of Jesus had to be done underground.

Soon after our arrival, our friends living in China were contacted by a Christian organization, which informed us that an itinerant Chinese minister had left the security of his government-supplied job to devote himself full time to sharing the gospel. As a result, two young women from a neighboring village surrendered their lives to Jesus and wanted to be baptized. But where could they be baptized? Their homes had no tubs, church buildings didn't exist, and it was incredibly cold, so the lakes and rivers were not an option. Could we somehow provide a means for these women to be baptized?

Our solution was to rent a cheap hotel room with a tub. I'll admit, I had a bit of an adrenaline rush doing something illegal for Jesus. There was something intensely beautiful about softly whispering the words to "Amazing Grace" with a handful of strangers while kneeling around a bathtub baptism. This time we weren't sitting in rows *or* circles, and there were no snacks offered before *or* after. This was something entirely different and yet somehow the same. It was as if God's presence was thicker and more palpable the further we ventured from the things that were familiar. I was beginning to see that God had a way of meeting us in the margins.

The purity of these two overseas experiences—one in Hungary and one in China—forever changed how I viewed what it means to be a church. When I later came back to the United States, I knew I wanted to pursue a life of ministry. I wanted more of that raw Kingdom of Heaven fire in my daily life. I didn't know how to articulate it then, but what I really wanted was access to the chaotic side of church. So, I did what seemed at the time like a logical next step—I went to Bible college. And it was horrible. Don't get me wrong. I had fun, the professors were great people, and the teaching was solid. But it didn't speak to the reality I had experienced overseas.

What I didn't know then is that the Bible college was a structure that trained leaders almost exclusively for the order side of church. Any mention of something messy or chaotic was met with caution and apprehension. I was beginning to see the friction that these two sides of the church produced and would continue to produce for the rest of my ministry life. All I knew was that I couldn't wait to get back on the mission field.

After graduation, Paulette, who was by then my wife, and I set out for the Philippines. I had no interest in starting a traditional church, an organization full of predictability. I wanted to find that other side of the church again—the holy chaos side. I wanted to be a part of something messy. Something real. Something risky. And I wanted to launch other people into the adventure of holy chaos as well. Little did I know that God was about to expose me to the biggest spiritual launching pad I'd ever known.

A Different Yet Similar Church in the Philippines

The Philippines was a perfect fit for us. The people were joyful and receptive, and it was here that I developed some of my closest friendships. But perhaps the greatest gift this island in the South China Sea gave me was yet another paradigm shift in my understanding of church. To help you understand my discovery, it's important to know the context of what life in the Philippines was like. At the time, there were few or no job options in the country. Consequently, over 90 percent of Filipino college graduates found employment outside of the Philippines. Most of them landed in places that were considered unreached by the gospel. Somehow, I had stumbled on a missionary-sending goldmine. The number one export of the Philippines was not bananas or pineapples—it was people! How exciting to set up a church on a college campus where new believers would head out into places that had never heard about Jesus! This was the groundswell of a spiritual firestorm.

I was thrilled, but not without reservations. My mind was flooded with questions. Is a church even a church if all its members are eventually sent away? Was this allowed? What would my financial supporters think? I could hear critics from back home in my head. "How are you making sure these students are having a multi-generational experience? You know church isn't church without older mentors, without elders, without a creed, without by-laws, without—fill in the blank." I too had questions, but as I looked around, it was clear that there wasn't enough order to replicate what was common back home. There were no elders to pick. We didn't have preachers. We didn't even have a curriculum. But that didn't seem to hinder the fact that Godly fruit was all around us. And these fruit-filled people were replicating themselves in the surrounding countries.

My connection to the ministry in the Philippines runs deep to this day. Over the years, this single campus ministry has grown to four campuses, and there have been hundreds if not thousands of students sent to countries such as Egypt, India, Malaysia, and beyond. This was now my third ministry setting in as many countries. With each paradigm shift, I was now slowly piecing together commonalities from each setting. As this new picture came into focus, I began to see the church in a whole new way.

I'm Not the Only One

This second side of the church is not new. Many others before me have discovered it and written about it. Most of these in recent decades have been missionaries who, like me, had overseas experiences that burned away the fog. One of these was Roland Allen, a missionary to China in the early 1900s. In 1927, he wrote a pamphlet called *The Spontaneous Expansion of the Church*. Here is what he had to say to the Western church:

> *We of today are enamored with organization; we pride ourselves on our skill in designing and directing it, but*

> when we are dealing with the propagation of the Gospel,
> our love for it leads us into serious dangers. It leads us to
> give material an undue importance; it leads us to attempt
> to organize spiritual forces.³

I love this. It shows that the West has been fixated on one side of the church for a very long time. Allen is not suggesting that we exchange one side of church for the other—that we embrace chaos over order. He is merely highlighting the dangers of embracing only order. Instead, he and others4 who have written about this invite us to embrace both sides of the church, because when we balance the tension between them, it sparks a spiritual fire that can ignite a gospel movement.

There are numerous examples of gospel movements overseas that have produced hundreds of thousands of new followers within just a few years. And that's not a typo.5Compare that to Christian life here in the US, where we consider it a success if we just maintain our church attendance levels from one year to the next. Such phenomenal growth is hard for most of us in the West to get our heads around. It seems like it must be a mistake or an anomaly at best. However, I think the truth is that we have been so programmed to see church as an institution that we can no longer even imagine ourselves as spiritual fire starters. In the name of peace and order, we have avoided the friction necessary to start godly movements.

In addition to Roland Allen, perhaps the one person who brought the most clarity to this two-sided dynamic of the church was a man named Ralph Winter. Ralph earned degrees from Cal Tech, Columbia, Cornell, and Princeton. He and his wife, Roberta, were missionaries for ten years in Guatemala. Upon their return to the United States, Ralph directly

---

3 Roland Allen, *The Spontaneous Expansion of the Church: And the Causes Which Hinder It* (Yuma, CO: Jawbone Digital, 2018), 117.
4 Two other writers of note include Donald McGavran and George Patterson. Donald McGavran was a missionary to India and in 1955 wrote *The Bridges of God.* George Patterson was a missionary to Honduras and wrote *The Church Multiplication Guide* in 1993.
5 2414now.net

influenced over 1,000 missionaries through his ground-breaking course, "The History of the Christian Movement." Many believe his most profound contribution was an address he delivered in 1973 to the All-Asia Mission Consultation in Seoul, South Korea. The transcript was later adapted into an article titled *The Two Structures of God's Redemptive Mission*. In it, he introduced the concept of a second side of church! He beautifully articulates what I had seen and experienced for years but for which I had no words. He identified the two sides of the church with these terms: modality and sodality.

Modality is the side of the church with which we are most familiar. It is the local and orderly side, on which we have a building, ministry programs, and paid staff. *Sodality* is the side of church that is more organic, where there is experimentation and chaos. It's here that the church takes on new shapes and forms. In that sense, the sodality side of the church moves like water. It's the side of the church that succumbs to a spiritual gravitational pull, being led into the crevices of society that need it most. Turns out, I wasn't the only one who felt like we were missing half the church!

Chaordic Tension

This relationship between chaos and order is not unique to the church. Visa's founder, Dee W. Hock, described the tug of war between chaos and order in organizations when he combined the two words and coined the phrase *chaordic tension*. In his book, *Birth of the Chaordic Age*, Hock highlighted the spectrum that all organizations operate under. Collapse, chaos, order, and control.

Just as businesses and organizations move progressively toward order and control as they become more established, so it is with the church. I experienced something unique and beautiful in Hungary, China, and the Philippines because the absence of an established order required our team to experiment and innovate—we had no choice but to operate in divine chaos.

In *The Two Structures of God's Redemptive Mission*, Ralph Winter not only described the two sides of church and the necessity for each but also addressed the structures that support these sides of church. I can now see that the reason I was drawn to campus ministry upon my return to the US was because I saw it as a training ground for experimentation in the chaos. Campus ministry is a natural sodalic structure designed to innovate by releasing change agents into the world. Institutions such as Bible colleges, as I found out, are modalic structures whose primary purpose is to train preachers and teachers for the order side of church. To be clear, sodality alone is an expression of the church, but it has limitations. Likewise, modality alone is also an expression of the church, but it too has limitations, albeit in entirely different ways.

In his book, *Beyond the Local Church*, missions leader Sam Metcalf likens sodality by itself to an army with casualties. While ground is being taken for the kingdom, the people taking that ground are not being cared for. Conversely, modality by itself will ultimately look more like a hospital for the hurting. Members of this church will likely grow old together but never expand. We can't keep these two sides of the church separate! We need both. We need chaordic tension. But how?

I believe the answer may be as simple as listening to the people of God sitting next to us in the pew. That's because God, in his infinite wisdom, has embedded a divine chaordic tension within his people. And one of the ways that tension expresses itself is in our spiritual gifts.

As we explored in Chapter 5, there are five distinct spiritual gifts and roles God has given us: apostles, prophets, evangelists, shepherds, and teachers. Generally speaking, it's the apostles and prophets who live on the margins of sodality. These are the ones who pioneer and experiment in the chaos. Conversely, it is often the shepherds and teachers who are most at home in the predictability and order of modality. And then there are the evangelists, who tend to operate comfortably on both sides.

Here is the problem. We tend to migrate to people who are wired the same way we are. In doing so, we avoid the spiritual tension and friction necessary to spark kingdom fires. That is why I challenged you at the end of Chapter 5 to recognize and foster the spiritual gifts in those around you. I'm a firm believer that it is just as important to know how you are *not* wired as it is to know how you *are*. And when you not only appreciate but also partner with those who are different from you, you advance the kingdom.

Developing a healthy appreciation for those who are different doesn't come naturally to most of us, but it is where the friction of fire building begins. Most ministry disagreements in church stem from someone on one side suggesting expansion (chaos), while someone on the other side argues that we need to first care for ourselves(order). But it is only when we recognize and appreciate those across the aisle that we have what we need to spark spiritual fires. If we remain clumped with those who think and operate like us, we will continue to see teachers limited to Bible churches, shepherds limited to community churches, prophets limited to charismatic churches, apostles limited to parachurch organizations, and evangelists sprinkled throughout.

So, how are you wired? What side of church do you lean toward? Who on the other side do you need to recognize, appreciate, and maybe even collaborate with? To help you answer those questions, I've created a chart of characteristics that briefly summarizes both the sodality and modality sides of church. As you review the two lists, consider which side of the chart you relate to the most.

Characteristics of the Two Sides of Church

Sodality (Chaos)	Modality (Order)
Mobile	Stationary
Takes new ground	Protects existing ground
Reproduces easily	Does not reproduce easily
Decentralized	Centralized
Narrow focus "there" (go to kids, homeless, etc.)	Broad focus "here" (bring people to our gym, library, and kitchen)
Pioneering	Established
Expansion driven	Care driven

Both sets of characteristics are necessary for the church to flourish, so there's no right or wrong answer when it comes to which side you gravitate toward. The important thing is to gain a healthy appreciation for the side you don't gravitate toward. Once you have an idea of which side of the church you're on, it's time to challenge yourself by taking the next step.

What's This Mean for You?

It's one thing to compare and contrast the megachurch in your city to the messy and organic church in an African slum. But what about the tension that lies within your immediate setting? What about your mom's group at the park or the book club in your break room? Although these settings may feel nothing like church, it doesn't mean they aren't. As a matter of fact, it's hard to imagine how every first-century church wouldn't have started in a similarly inconspicuous way. Even as I listen to the origin stories of well-established churches today, most of them started with a small group of people with a missional mindset. It's only a matter of time before these once small and outward-facing groups are faced with the inevitable temptation to succumb to comfort and familiarity. So how do we maintain this tension?

Recently, me and a few other experienced ministers decided to tackle this problem by partnering with those few innovators that have shown a propensity to start spiritual fires in their communities. Most of these people are apostolic types that we have nicknamed spiritual entrepreneurs. We've noticed that even these naturally gifted fire starters need a framework to keep the chaordic tension alive. What we discovered is that if we wanted to create a new paradigm, we would need new mental pictures. We intentionally chose something incredibly simple and common. Something that everyone could easily grasp its meaning. What we landed on were "dugouts" and "playgrounds."

The term "playground" reinforces the playful attitude necessary to keep getting outside. It keeps those opportunistic environments alive for missional experimentation. While dugouts remain those modalic places where we replenish and refill before we are sent back out, what we learned is that these new terms go a long way in helping these early-developing ministries, ones like yours, to keep from falling into some of the traps of those who have gone before them. Traps of insultation and isolation.

A word to the sodalic. If you resonate with the characteristics on the sodalic (chaos) side of the chart, I encourage you to experiment and innovate as you live out your mission. If you wait for approval or a budget from some committee, chances are good you will be waiting for a long time and become frustrated. The people who hold the money and the power are typically modalic. This is often a good thing because it keeps those who thrive in chaos from making rash decisions. Part of your challenge is to win them over with actions, not words. While modalic people tend to be cautious when it comes to expansion, they won't ignore positive stories happening in their midst. Spiritual fruit doesn't lie. However, you won't have a story worth sharing until you've experimented for a while, so start small and let God grow your idea. There is a high probability that your original idea will shift a few times. This may bring caution and scrutiny from the modalic side, but trust the process. Your diligence will pay off when the people in power see evidence of long-standing obedience in the same direction.

A word to the modalic. If you resonate with the characteristics on the modalic (order) side of the chart, find ways to multiply truth and care among the individuals within your group. This can only happen through the grassroots discipleship process modeled by Jesus. When it comes to developing a scalable, healthy environment, there is no substitute for discipleship. We must resist the temptation to embrace any quick fixes.

If teaching is your primary gift, resist the temptation to be the sole mouthpiece for your group. If shepherding is your primary gift, resist the temptation to carry the emotional weight of everyone around you. Once you devote yourself to replicating disciples who can teach and care for one another, stability will emerge. Not a perfect environment, but stable nonetheless. It's at this point that you must turn your attention outward by embracing the pioneers in your life. I know these chaotic people can be frustrating, but the key to keeping the movement of a firestorm growing, is largely dependent on your ability to release the pioneers. You likely won't have a hard time remembering to keep the spiritual fire healthy and strong within your community, but it's also your job to honor those who are attempting to start new fires. You honor them when you both affirm their gifts and provide structure and guidelines for acting on a new idea. Those who can "manage this tension" well hold the key to unlocking a movement of our own here in the States. For the brave souls who dare to try, a beautiful gift awaits. A mesmerizing and refining fire that spreads effortlessly throughout your town, transforming all that bask in its glow.

PART 4   PERMISSION TO START FIRES: DEVELOPING CONTAGIOUS ASPIRATION

12. FIRE REQUIRES CHEMISTRY

My friend, Dan Hubbard, wrote a song called "*Heaven in My Backyard*," in which he dialogues with his brother, who now resides in heaven. The lyrics describe a beautiful moment in which a slice of heaven is lived out here on earth. Experiencing such moments isn't a common occurrence for most of us. Yet, even in our broken, busy, and hectic world, I believe most of us have seen at least a glimmer of something so beautiful, selfless, and magical that we know it's not of this earth. It's a culmination of things, a kind of chemistry unleashing what the scriptures refer to as "the mystery." It might happen when forgiveness miraculously restores a broken relationship, when a sacrificial act saves a life, or when a transcendent experience of worship ushers us into the presence of God. Such moments often catch us off guard. We have no idea how they happened, we just feel incredibly fortunate and hope that we may one day experience something like them again.

Would it surprise you if I said that such moments aren't actually as random as they might seem? I've been fortunate enough to be part of a community in which heaven-on-earth experiences were a routine part of the culture. Having lived and ministered in that community for over two decades, I now understand that there were some key components at work—a kind of chemistry that catalyzed spiritual fires among us. I believe anyone, including you, can employ those same components to create a similar culture where spiritual chemistry is alive and active. In an attempt to give you a picture of what a kingdom of heaven environment looks like, I'm inviting you to take a walk with me through a memory from my campus ministry days.

A Picture of Heaven on Earth

It's 10:30 p.m. on a Monday night in October, and I'm about to enter the most energy-filled event in town. It's not at a frat house, concert hall or bar. It's in a small brick building that looks more like a dentist's office than a party house. There's also a cross embedded in the brick, which adds to the stale and stuffy vibe. However, what the building lacks in aesthetics, it makes up for in location. It's directly across the street from the center of campus, within walking distance for any and all students.

We refer to this building as the campus house. Again, not very exciting. For as much energy as our gatherings in this place produce, you might think we'd have a better name for it. A few years back, one of the students shortened "campus house" to "Chouse," and it stuck. I guess that's better. The Chouse has a large open room that accommodates about 100 college students, with spillover room for another forty. I know this because we regularly pushed the occupancy limits.

As I approach the front steps, the buzz spills out from the inside, a mixture of conversation and laughter. I walk in, and the energy seems even thicker. It's crowded, and I can feel the room temperature rise. I estimate there to be about ninety in attendance. Just then, someone across the room yells my name over the crowd. I don't know who it is, but it sure feels nice. This feeling of inclusion and belonging is something we all deeply value. It's a core value that has somehow seeped into our culture. This place feels more like a party on a Friday night than a Christian gathering on a Monday night. On more than one occasion, students have wandered in off the street, asking where the keg is. I love it when that happens.

I'm looking for a student named Ashley. This is her party, by the way. I hate to admit it, but I'm not entirely sure what she looks like. These college kids are all starting to look the same to me! I should know, though. After all, we met for an hour last Thursday to set up this party. I'm almost positive I saw her at our worship gathering earlier tonight. I'm pretty sure she was sitting in the front row of the campus auditorium and wearing a pink hat.

My eyes start scanning the room. *Pink hat, pink hat, pink* . . . There she is, sitting on the couch with three of her closest friends. I take a step toward her when I hear my name again. "Pete!" I turn to see Corey, one of my student leaders, beaming with excitement. He has a friend by his side, and even though Corey is right next to me, he yells—partly because of the noise but mostly out of excitement.

"You know Dave, my roommate I told you about?" Of course, I did. Corey and I had talked about Dave's spiritual questions at length in my office last Wednesday. Or was it Tuesday? Anyway, he yells again, "He has something to tell you!"

I turn my attention to Dave. The look in his eyes is pure peace. A look that comes only from going through a wrestling match with God and coming out both surrendered and victorious on the other side. I knew what he was going to ask me, and this was the kind of moment I had grown addicted to.

"Um, Mr. Cocco? Do you think I could get baptized tonight too?"

Yes! Now, it wasn't just Ashley's party; it was Dave's as well. I ask Corey and Dave to follow me. We swing by to pick up Ashley and her friend, Jamie from the couch. The five of us work our way through the crowd into a back office, where I lay out the details of what will happen next. I've done this so many times before, I could do it in my sleep. But it never gets old.

"Alright, I'm not baptizing anyone tonight," I say. Then I look into the eyes of Corey and Jamie, the two who were not there to be baptized, and address them specifically, "You have contributed more to these two lives than I have, and you should be the ones to baptize your friends."

This is such a powerful moment. It's where all four of these students become major players in the kingdom, perhaps for the first time. I instruct Corey and Jamie to address the crowd and simply tell of the events that led their friends to this beautiful place of surrender. I remind them that this isn't about them and encourage them to make God the hero in everything they say. I can see a bit of relief come over them as they nod in agreement. Some of that relief comes from clarity, but most of it comes from an acknowledgement that this really isn't about them; it's about God. It's his story, and they are just entering into it. It's beautiful.

As we return to the main room, there are now well over 100 students sitting cross-legged on the floor waiting for the party's main event. The room feels hot and sweaty, but every eye is glued on Dave and Ashley, and every ear is tuned to their stories. I sit in the back, scanning the now-silent room. The intensity of the Holy Spirit's presence is rising. I offer a quick prayer, asking for His divine presence to settle on these hearts. I can tangibly feel God doing his part. I fully anticipate conviction to settle in the room, prompting even more to surrender their lives to Jesus and be baptized, while still others will become baptizers at a future party.

The evening ends with two soaking-wet students standing in front of a horse trough full of water. They are wrapped in towels and surrounded by over 100 of their closest friends, all of whom are laying hands on one another in prayer. I'm convinced it's the closest thing to heaven I'll ever experience. The night is incredible. Afterward, I head home and go to bed full of contentment, knowing that the stories we heard and the surrender these students displayed will lead to additional conversations this week—and perhaps to another party next Monday.

Sometimes a guest or two who were not college students attended our Monday night celebrations; parents and family members, mostly. After experiencing one of our baptism parties, their response was always the same: "This is different from what I experience at my church." I once had an alum come back to visit one of our baptism nights after more than twenty years. "I forgot what this was like," he said. It was a sad statement, but I had to agree that there was something about this setting that was special. Something that baptisms at my local church didn't seem to quite have. But what was it? There had to be something more.

The Chemistry of Worship, Community, and Mission

Although I initially had a hard time understanding why this heaven-on-earth purity I experienced at our baptism parties was so difficult to find elsewhere, I now understand that it wasn't so much a product of youthful energy as it was divine chemistry. There were three key elements present that created a reaction. Specifically, those elements were worship, community, and mission. I'll come back to those elements shortly, but first, it may help to understand some basics about how chemistry works.

In chemistry, certain elements become "reactants" when combined. A reactant is simply a raw material that undergoes a change when combined with other elements. However, a catalyst is required. In the scientific world, hydrogen—a colorless, odorless, tasteless, but highly combustible gas—is a common catalyst. Almost all metals and nonmetals react with hydrogen at high temperatures. And just as an invisible component like hydrogen creates catalytic reactions in the material world, the Holy Spirit, who can't be seen, is a catalyst in the spiritual realm. It is the catalytic presence of the Holy Spirit that transforms a boring brick building into a church that throws dynamic baptism parties.

Most of us operate under the assumption that the Holy Spirit works independently of our involvement. While this is true in some ways, it's also been my experience that the Holy Spirit, like hydrogen, does its best catalytic work by interacting with elements we have a part in providing. Instead of assuming that the Holy Spirit doesn't really need us, we need to understand that we have a role in catalyzing spiritual reactions. We may not be able to cause the reaction on our own, but we can put the right elements together. In that sense, we are co-chemists with the Holy Spirit, and it's up to us to put the right elements in the petri dish. So, what are those elements?

Initially, there may seem to be an overwhelming number of elements to choose from, especially when thinking about the traditional church. After all, the church does so many things! There are small groups, service projects, prayer meetings, and mission committees. Not to mention worship services, softball leagues, and potlucks. But if we think in terms of categories, I propose that there are only three: worship, community, and mission. If we made an exhaustive list of everything the church is and does and then boiled it all down, these three would remain.

Worship is more than singing, community is more than attending a small group; and mission is more than a trip. It might be more accurate to say that worship is surrendering to the notion that God is big and I am not. Community is sharing the fullness of our lives with others, and mission is pursuing what should and could be but isn't. It's this beautiful combination of worship, community, and mission—or Jesus, friends, and adventure—that the Holy Spirit of God catalyzes into experiences of heaven on earth. Did you note the word "combination" in that sentence? It's the *combination* or overlap of all three components that the Holy Spirit catalyzes into divine magic. When we fixate on just one or two of these components, we may end up with some good outcomes but fall short of the slice of heaven on earth we're hoping for. And if it's a divine chemical reaction we're after, I'd like to suggest that the order in which we combine the components matters.

We Must Lead with Mission

For many of us, there is an assumption that if I'm going to carry out a godly personal mission, the first component must be worship. However, when we start with worship, the outcome is usually a controlled experience that takes place at a specific location at a set time. When a worship experience is what everything is organized around, community and mission are not always easy to add to the mix. That's because a worship environment is typically experienced with other believers in a modalic setting. Trying to move from a place of comfort and control is never easy. In our traditional churches, it's not uncommon for these controlled environments to feel so comfortable that it's even a challenge to interact with the people in the pews. I've personally gone through years of church attendance without knowing the people sitting right next to me. Worship was strong, but community was lacking. Using worship to build community may sound right, but once you attend a Super Bowl party awkwardly hosted at the church building, you'll likely rethink your position.

Unfortunately, mission is then even harder to add than community. If talking to our fellow church attendees is a challenge, then expecting those same worship attendees to be missionaries to their neighborhoods is nearly impossible. That's why I believe worship shouldn't be the first component in the petri dish.

On campus, we too had a worship service, but community was our first component in the petri dish. I'd like to think that we were bucking the pressures of traditional church culture by prioritizing community, but it's closer to the truth to admit that community found us. There were twenty thousand students between the ages of nineteen and twenty-two on our campus. They all lived within the same square mile, and none of them had marriage problems or kids. It was community on steroids. Organizing our church around community was the natural thing to do. Adding worship as our second element in the petri dish came quite naturally, but adding the third element of mission was still a challenge. The combination of community and worship readily attracted more Christians. The results felt good, and our ministry grew. But without a clear mission, our focus was sometimes directed more inward than outward. It was in such seasons that our staff felt more like counselors than disciple makers.

I think this inward-focused dynamic describes most growing churches. Maybe even yours. The emphasis on community and worship is strong and attracts other Christians, but without a clear mission, there's a danger of becoming a magnet for the needy or a platform for debates. Even small groups have a tendency to turn inward over time. Again, building a personal mission around community may feel right, but if there is no clear outward mission, this community will eventually dissolve. We are all built to fulfill an outward mission, and I often say that if your community doesn't formulate a mission, then it will be formulated for you. Which is likely to take the form of conflict or drama.

Trying to add the element of mission almost never works. The Christian culture that is created by worship and community is often so strong that we tend to adopt the wrong mission. We begin to think that the whole point of being a Christian is for more people to be added to our community of worshipers. Meanwhile, the homeless are still on the streets, orphans are still abandoned, and refugees are still ignored. This is the cruise passenger mentality we talked about in Chapter 7. Community and worship may grow our church with more people who look like us, but in doing so, we run the risk of being the very thing Jesus despised. Pharisees who *protect* what they have rather than *share* what they have.

So, all of these reasons and more are why I believe we need to organize ourselves first around mission rather than worship or community. And this is another way in which the second side of church plays a part. If modality is the orderly side of church, it makes sense to assume that this is where worship and community operate. If sodality is the chaotic side of church where we pioneer and explore, then it makes sense to assume that this is where mission operates. The point is, if we are going to put mission into the petri dish first, then we need to start with sodality. No church ever took new territory in a sanctuary, classroom, or boardroom. It always happens first on the fringes, out beyond the walls of the church. All three elements—worship, community, and mission—are necessary, but mission must lead.

It's the Overlap that Counts

Many people think, "My church already has all three—worship, community, and mission. We're doing pretty good." But here's the thing:

This isn't about whether your church has all three, but whether they overlap. In other words, is there spiritual chemistry among them?

Unfortunately, most of our traditional churches have separated these three components. Worship is largely experienced in a Sunday morning time slot. Community is reserved for a midweek small group. And for the few who want to make an impact on the world, there is an annual mission trip next July. When separated, these components lose the kinetic power and life-changing energy for which the church should be known. It is only when all three parts overlap and are catalyzed by the Holy Spirit that we experience the contagious aspiration of the kingdom of God. Sometimes we stumble on this overlap without really trying, and it's almost always on a mission trip.

I got a reminder of this when I recently served as the interim minister of a local congregation. One Sunday morning, the leader of a recent mission trip to Mexico gave a report about the trip to the congregation. He talked about how the team had gone to Mexico to build a house (a mission). He described how special it was for three generations—grandpa, dad, and son—to participate in this trip (community). He then mentioned how one day, while working on the roof of the house, they heard a familiar worship song being played in the house next door. When those three components came together in his mind, he was overcome with emotion and immediately began to cry.

As I listened to his report, it all made sense. Church at its best isn't about checking off a to-do list; it's chemistry. It's that inexplicable mystery that happens when mission, community, and worship overlap. It's a catalytic spiritual energy that can only come from the Holy Spirit, and the result is almost always a tenderness of heart with tears running down a face. Beautiful, inexplicable tears. That's what made Monday baptism parties at the Chouse so special. Even though we didn't understand the intricacies of this dynamic, we knew enough to recreate a catalytic environment for worship, community, and mission to collide. Anything less just felt like a counterfeit. Now that I have terms for these components and a procedure to implement them, I can more easily identify why some environments feel a little off. Environments that may bring value and may be helpful, but that you intuitively know are not the full version of the kingdom of heaven on earth.

When we experience only two components in the petri dish, we are left with a generic version of the church. If we experience mission and worship without community, we are left with something transactional, like a stranger sharing a tract or witnessing at your door. When we experience mission and community without worship, it tends to be a social justice trip. Again, it may be helpful, but it isn't the fullest expression of the church. And when we experience community and worship without mission, it tends to resemble a dinner club where overtime we grow tired of seeing the same faces, sitting in the same circles, and, hearing the same stories until we eventually ask, "Why are we here?"

In order to keep your personal mission from feeling a bit off, here are a few questions that may be helpful for you to routinely ask yourself. Which component is most lacking in my personal mission? Worship, community, or mission? How can I implement that lacking or missing component without compromising the others? And perhaps the most important question of all is: What component is my personal mission organized around?

Organizing around Mission

Organizing around a mission may be easier than you think. It starts by asking this question: "What could and should be, but isn't?" Remember, a compelling mission that captures the attention of all involved will be easily understood and almost never spiritual in its description. Maybe it's stable housing for refugees or internship opportunities for students from under-resourced communities. However, if that same mission has no room for the presence of God (worship), it too will feel a bit wonky and powerless. I'm only pointing out that mission must lead the way, and like we mentioned in Chapter 3, our dream should be big enough to scratch the itch of all involved. Christian and non-Christian. We need to trust that God is just as present when we work to meet the tangible needs of the community as he is when we sing to him in worship on the weekends. In fact, it seems like the personal mission stories where God shows up the strongest are in the midst of secular organizations that encompass a wide audience sharing a deep belief.

What if the church was known for coming alongside the existing missions in our cities? One that everyone agrees with? What if we became known as the fuel that finishes their work? And what about you? What if your personal mission was to lock arms with non-Christians, accomplishing something you both care about?

When I was in campus ministry, one of our best decisions was to stop creating our own mission trips so we could join in on trips others were already doing. This idea came from one of our students. Phil came to our ministry as a junior. He transferred from the University of Minnesota, where he was involved with a student-led group that held "Pay It Forward Tours." The idea was to fill a bus with students who would travel across the country during spring break and serve various communities along the way. This organization masterfully combined the bonding element of a road trip with meaningful and selfless service opportunities. It was a trip designed for students from all backgrounds, which made it a perfect fit for a campus ministry such as ours. In essence, it was a double mission trip. Not only would we serve the needs of those in several communities, but we would do it with people who were not followers of Jesus.

Here's how it worked: The students might serve food at a homeless shelter in Indiana on Monday, pick up garbage on a Tuesday in Kentucky, do roof repair in Tennessee on Wednesday, and so on. At the end of the week, they'd meet up with other buses from other schools in the same location for a big celebration before returning home. The point wasn't so much about getting to the destination as it was about embracing the journey. It was brilliant.

What Phil brought to our ministry was such a success that we committed to making this trip a top priority every year. What we stumbled on in that experiment was not just how powerful it was to send Christians on a trip. (After all, every youth group in the world was already doing that.) But rather, the intent was to send Christians to accomplish a mission alongside non-Christians. This was how we organized ourselves around a mission. Mission was the first component in the petri dish, and the community came along for the ride (literally). The third component, worship, was the only missing element, and we found that this piece came much more naturally than we had anticipated.

Our students were not trained to convert others; they were only encouraged to be honest and to let their godly purpose for serving shine. After spending hours together serving others, the bus ride to the next destination gave our students an opportunity to share why they were there. Inevitably, there was a contingent of non-Christian students whose interest was piqued by this small community within a community that was fueled by something divine. I doubt any of our students on that bus recognized how worship, community, and mission were being catalyzed by the Holy Spirit. To them, it wasn't a formula. It was just a supernatural experience of heaven on earth, in which God did things that amazed them all.

Even though the goal of the trip was never to boost our numbers back on campus, attendance at our Monday night worship service inevitably spiked on their return. Those Mondays felt a lot like baptism parties because we were once again reaping the benefits of a church that was birthed outside of our walls. In this case, a church born on a bus.

I loved listening to the non-Christian students from the bus trip who attended our Monday night service and claimed that it was their first experience of church. I'd nod and give a wry smile. "First experience with church, huh?" I didn't feel the need to explain, but I knew a fuller story—it was at least their second.

PART 5

PERMISSION TO PRIORITIZE PLAY: DEVELOPING CREATIVE INITIATIVE

Inspiration exists, but it has to find you moving.
—Pablo Picasso

In some ways, we are ending this book in the same place we started. By continuing to develop your creative initiative. That's because your personal mission is never static. You never know what amazing opportunity is just around the corner. This is what makes life fun. Don't let the seriousness of life insulate you from the ever-evolving personal mission God has you on. The moment you close yourself off from new possibilities, your life will turn inward, protecting what you have and losing out on one of life's greatest joys—play. That's why prioritizing play is so important. Sure, the stakes are high and aspects of your mission may be weighty, but without an atmosphere of play, it becomes very difficult to experiment, which is a primary tool required to push your missional life forward.

I learned my first lessons about the connection between play and experimentation from my grandfather. Nearly every Sunday of my youth was spent at my grandparents' house. Like many other families, we ate a big lunch after church and settled onto the couch to watch whatever game was playing on television. At some point in the late afternoon, my brother or I would give Grandpa the eye, a look that said, "It's time." He'd nod in response, and off we'd go. Where he took us next proved to be the most beneficial training ground for playful experimentation I would ever know.

Week after week, year after year, Grandpa walked us boys down his long-sloped backyard to a small lake where a little rowboat was tied to a dock. We'd push out from shore, and within moments we entered our bliss. Fishing was our shared obsession. We all loved it. It was our playground, but that didn't mean it was easy. Grandpa taught us that we couldn't just throw out our line and hope for the best; we had to experiment to find what worked. Even though that required work, Grandpa had a way of making it feel like play. He helped us think through all the factors, such as water depth and temperature, time of year and time of day, and whether it was overcast or sunny. Then there were all the options we held in our hands. What weight of fishing line should we use? What lures? What colors? What retrieval methods? There was an endless amount of experimenting to be done. There were no YouTube videos where we could learn hacks or shortcuts. We had to figure things out through trial and error, which was a gift. A gift that ignited a passion for fishing that has stayed with me to this day. Catching fish is always fun, but it's the ongoing experimentation that aligns my heart with the old adage, "The worst day fishing is better than the best day working."

Experimenting within God's kingdom isn't all that different from fishing. Namely, we tend to start out with a healthy dose of optimism. We are energized by the possibility of catching the proverbial "big one," whatever that may be within our context. But in every missional endeavor—and I do mean *every*—there comes an experience or even a season of what Grandpa called "getting skunked." For all your enthusiasm, patience, and hard work, inevitably there will be times you come up empty. That's when you will be most tempted to quit.

Pursuing and sustaining a personal mission isn't for the faint of heart because there are no foolproof formulas. Which is another reason why it's so important to focus not just on fulfilling our mission but also on enjoying the process along the way. This is the key to longevity. If you want to develop a personal mission that lasts, you must learn to prioritize play.

13. PLAY ON A TEAM

As a young person, basketball was my passion. I played every day. I couldn't get enough. My first thought each morning as I lifted my head from the pillow was where I would play my next game. Tuesday and Thursday nights, I played with my buddies at the church gym. On Sundays, I was with the older guys at the high school. On the other days, I played pick-up games at the local park, and occasionally I even drove across town to play at the recreation center.

As it was with fishing, there were plenty of factors to consider when it came to my experiments with basketball. Were we playing indoors or outside? Full court or half court? How many were playing? How experienced was my competition? Of course, all of these variables mattered, but to what end? Was winning the only goal? As it turns out, no. It took me years to articulate this, but I can now see what I think my grandpa saw as he walked us down his sloped back yard each Sunday—purposeful comradery. A mission, no matter how trivial or noble, just isn't as fun without teammates.

Of course, it is entirely possible to win without even knowing your teammates names, but to surround yourself with your most intimate friends who have no interest in winning isn't fun either. All of us need both comradery and a clear objective. To do things alone leaves you empty, but not keeping score feels pointless.

As you might have guessed, a similar principle applies as you pursue your personal mission. You need to play hard to win, which is to achieve your mission; *and* you need to play well with others, which is to invest in your teammates.

Discipleship Is the Real Game

Over time, I realized that the real game—in basketball and in all facets of my life—was to develop my teammates. It became my passion to help those around me value the combination of winning as well as enjoying the ups and downs of getting there. What I discovered is that most people are quick to nod in agreement that both success and comradery are essential, but they show their true colors once you put them in the proverbial game. That's when it becomes clear that some people want to win so badly that they're willing to sacrifice relationships, and others are so relationship-focused that they don't even want to keep score. Both extremes are immensely discouraging.

Keeping with the basketball analogy, I can still remember what turned out to be the most frustrating game I ever played. I was on a mission trip and playing with a mixed group of young men and women from our US and Philippine campus ministries. The Filipinos were perfectly content to gleefully run about, holding the ball without dribbling. Simultaneously, one of our highly competitive American students was so fixated on winning that he was cursing while throwing elbows against female players who were much smaller than him.

It was one of those moments in which I faced a choice. I could throw up my hands in frustration and walk away (a very tempting option), or I could make this a discipleship opportunity. And by "discipleship," I mean on-the-job training, because those who join our teams are entering into an apprenticeship. Everyone playing that day was partnering in my personal mission to empower tomorrow's leaders. Although a basketball game may have seemed insignificant or unrelated to that mission, it wasn't. I took what happened on the court that day as an opportunity to have one-on-one conversations with each person. I wanted them to understand the parallels between their behavior on the court and their approach to our mission. I wanted them to see that discipleship is the real game. I wanted them to understand that it is the moments of conflict that provide the best opportunities for growth. People just don't learn as much when everything is going well.

Whether your mission involves winning basketball games, housing the homeless, or providing a community for youth, discipling your teammates is ultimately the real game. If you want to have a long-lasting personal mission, you will need to reframe these frustrating moments by seeing them as discipleship opportunities.

The Big Win

In basketball, I learned to make a distinction between small wins and big wins. Small wins were those tangible things like outscoring my opponent or making a pinpoint pass. My big win was developing more quality teammates. A similar distinction you will need to make as you develop your personal mission.

Small wins are not insignificant; they are concrete goals that can be easily measured. For example, the number of people who are now employed, housed, or sober because of your mission. The bigger win, I would argue, is to see your teammates get a taste of what it could look like to develop their own personal missions. This is the goal of discipleship—making disciples who make disciples. Which means you have the responsibility to disciple whoever is in the game with you, especially any teammates who may not yet be believers.

When we have a compelling personal mission that meets the needs of those around us, it should attract a wide audience. Make sure to put these people to work, regardless of their spiritual affiliation. (Remember the "Pay-it-Forward" tour.) Discipleship is not an add-on course; it is the entire process. Unfortunately, the approach of getting people to believe *in* Jesus before we allow them to work *with* Jesus is all too common. It's been my experience that when people join a mission that has removed the spiritual hurdle, they are more likely to feel like they are entering a "no judgment" zone. It is in this safe context that people can be discipled without always knowing they are being discipled. A common phrase I picked up from my missionary friends is "to disciple *onto* conversion, not *after* conversion." Besides, people cannot be expected to commit to something they've never experienced, and they certainly can't be expected to become leaders of their own teams until they've played on someone else's team. Thus, it's imperative that we first get people in the game. It's the model Jesus set for us.

Jesus understood that in order for his faith-challenged teammates (disciples) to one day lead their own teams (personal missions), they first needed to be in the game with him for a while. So he took them along as he healed the sick and fed the hungry. It was only after they had been with him for a while that he sent them out two by two to minister on their own. And what was the instruction he gave? Freely you have received; freely give" (Matthew 10:5-8 niv). In other words, bless people by giving them what I've given you. "Freely you have received; freely give." That's what on-the-job discipleship is—to lock arms with a teammate and share your experience. But when it comes to selecting teammates, does that mean anyone will do?

Three Principles for Selecting the Right Teammates

Whether you are trying to establish a halfway house for those in transition or providing a culture appreciation night for the teens at your school, you need a team. Teams don't need to be big. In fact, the most effective teams are often quite small. The bigger the team, the slower and less agile it becomes. One or two teammates is all that's necessary, but if they are the wrong teammates, your mission could be quickly derailed. That's why it's crucial to select the right teammates. While you want your personal mission to remain open to all who want to join in, you will need to be much more selective when picking your founding partners. It may be good to review Chapter 4 as a reminder of how important good character is, not only in you but within your immediate teammates as well. As you evaluate the fruit in one's rearview mirror, here are three distinct characteristics to look for.

Faithfulness, availability, and teachability. There is a long list of organizations that use this FAT (faithful, available, and teachable) grid when selecting teammates, and with good reason. I've used this grid for many years now, and it is amazing how complete this trifecta is at separating the competent teammates from the rest. Here are just a few thoughts on each characteristic that may help you recognize the high-potential teammates that surround you.

Faithful: Here is a simple question to ask when looking for a teammate. "Who is known for sticking to it?" Specifically, who is known for sticking to their job, to their spouse, and to the promises they made? When selecting a teammate, you won't need the most skilled person, but you want to be with the person whose word is their bond. This will give you assurance that they won't leave when things get tough.

Available: Even the most faithful people won't be worth much if they don't have enough available hours in the day. One thing I've learned over the years is to not be so quick to assume that my desired person is too busy. Do yourself a favor and let them decide. If they meet the first criteria of being faithful, chances are they will give you an honest assessment of their availability. They won't want to let you down.

Teachable: For me, this has proven to be the most important characteristic. A culture of trust can only be built on the spirit of teachability. This includes you. As a leader, it's imperative that you sincerely listen. Your example will go a long way in creating an environment where shared input is the norm and where God can more easily be heard.

There are few things more exciting and life-giving than being on a team with the right teammates. It's a real gift to find those perfect few who share in your mission and have extraordinary clarity about what they do in relation to that mission. As your mission grows, it will be your job to protect your current team by rejecting the temptation to succumb to the counterfeit teams that dominate our Christian culture.

Counterfeit Teams
Gatherings

Gatherings are important. They are the best place for information to be declared and for corporate worship to be experienced. But gatherings were never intended to replace teams. As a matter of fact, they are supposed to support and empower teams within the gathering. The bigger the gathering, the more teams it should support. Instead of being known as a body that supports multiple outward teams, the church has become synonymous with one central gathering. Consequently, the default understanding of a win has been reduced to attending that gathering—and the higher the attendance number, the bigger the win. I have no problem with a church growing their gathering as long as they are also growing their teams. When a church becomes obsessed with the gathering, they are in danger of making that gathering a counterfeit team. This can be an extremely frustrating scenario for those wanting to make a kingdom impact—one that reminds me of an especially discouraging basketball experience from my youth.

I don't know if I can adequately describe the level of excitement I felt as a seventh grader when members of the eighth-grade team invited me to join them at a summer basketball camp. It was a rush just to be asked. To know that others recognized some level of skill seemed to infuse a confidence within me that directly increased my ball-playing abilities. In the days leading up to the camp, I had a hard time sleeping. I was constantly imagining the array of scenarios in which I might find myself on the court, including pinpoint passes and three-point shots. I couldn't wait to show these guys what I could do.

Now, try to imagine my immense disappointment when the leaders of the camp didn't give us time to play. Instead, they sat us in a large group on one end of the court and gave us lectures about the game. Don't get me wrong; the lectures were relevant, informative, and creative. We had guest speakers, including high school and college stars as well as successful coaches from the area. The information was top-notch. Occasionally, we even got to run some drills. We just never got to play an actual game.

It seems like we make this kind of mistake all the time. Whether it's in business, the church, or teaching our kids how to drive, we Westerners tend to migrate to preparatory lectures rather than hands-on engagement. Conferences, training sessions, and weekly worship services are fixated on giving us information before we get to practice anything. The sad reality about my basketball camp experience was how quickly the culture of the camp made us pupils instead of players. I guess this is what it means to be "institutionalized"—we just accept that it's best practice for information to precede action. However, I have found that the longer people are subjected to being trained and informed, the more likely they are to believe that this *is* the game. Whether sitting on one end of the gym or one end of the pew, instruction and information have a way of becoming the endgame.

It wasn't too long ago that people started choosing whether and where to attend church services based on the uniqueness of the information that was delivered. As a young minister, I felt pressured to give people content that would wow them. There was a massive push to inform people of something new rather than inspire them to act on something old. This obsession with content has been our reality ever since, and the results are that masses of people across our nation are being institutionalized into thinking that this is just how things are supposed to be. This is what happens when we see everyone in our congregations as pupils rather than players. We have to remember that God has designed his kingdom around everyone being a player in the kingdom game. He is both our coach and our star player, and our job is to play in ways that allow him to shine. The only way we lose is if we choose to settle for being an attendee at a gathering rather than a player in the game.

Instead of creating more gatherings for instruction, we need to focus our energies on creating more teams with players. Instruction is important, but it's only useful when applied to players.

Groups

Groups are smaller than gatherings and thus can give the appearance of being teams. However, the objective of a group is not to achieve a win but to socialize—to belong. While this is an important objective, it's still not a team. Groups don't rally around a common goal as much as they rally around a common interest. Whether it's watching the football game, catching a drink with a few coworkers at happy hour, or eating pot roast with family on Sunday afternoon, groups unite people with a common interest. It's a mistake to think that just because we share a common interest in something meaningful, it will produce a team. It turns out that there is a big difference between a common interest and a common goal.

Church small groups are notorious for this. People often feel a sense of purpose and optimism when starting a small group, only to find that it quickly fizzles out. Although the goal is that these groups will stand the test of time, the common interests around which they initially gather often isn't enough to hold them together for the long haul. In his book *The Forgotten Ways*, professor and mission strategist Alan Hirsch addresses this problem by suggesting that we tweak our common interest to include a common goal or mission. When people work together for the good of something or someone outside the group, they are less likely to plateau or disband. Instead, they develop what Hirsch calls *communitas*. While community is often manifested in an inward-focused group, *communitas* is always manifested in an outward-focused team. He writes:

> [*Communitas*] involves adventure and movement, and it describes that unique experience of togetherness that really happens only among a group of people inspired

by the vision of a better world actually attempting to do something about it.[6]

Teams Are the Mode for Movement

In Part 4, I stated that the three essential components for starting spiritual fires are worship, community, and mission. In this chapter, I've explored three kinds of assemblies: teams, groups, and gatherings. Now, I want to briefly comment on the relationship between these two sets of three.

Gatherings are easily organized around worship. Groups are easily organized around the community, and teams are easily organized around a mission. What might be the result if our groups and gatherings existed to serve our teams? How might things change if our small groups became support hubs for our small teams? Can you envision a church in which gatherings are not the focal point but inspirational settings in which we celebrate team victories?

The easiest place to integrate the overlap of worship, community, and mission is in the smallest assembly, which is the team. In addition, starting with the smallest assembly is the only way to successfully integrate worship, community, and mission into the larger assemblies of groups and gatherings. When small things grow, they reproduce their DNA. Just as families reproduce their biological DNA as they grow, churches do the same with their spiritual DNA. This DNA is naturally passed from small to large. From teams to groups to gatherings, not the other way around.

If we want to see a movement of God spread across our country and world, I believe the key is to activate multiple personal missions and empower small teams to carry them out. To do so, it's critical to understand that the church must function primarily as an organism, not an organization. When we start with gatherings, we take the organism out of the equation, forcing us to manage an organization from its inception. In

---
6 Alan Hirsch, *The Forgotten Ways: Reactivating Apostolic Movements*, Revised Edition (Grand Rapids, MI: Brazos Press, 2016), 315.

this scenario, Christians are not expected to *experiment* but to *take notes*. People are not expected to *disciple*, but to *get plugged in*. Members are not expected to *play in the game* but to *volunteer for the professionals*. As a gathering grows, more and more is required from the members to sustain it. Large gatherings require lots of volunteer hours and lots of money. Staff and programs become the preeminent contributors to growth, and thus finances and volunteers quickly become the most desired resources. When the bulk of our time and money is spent on keeping the machine running, we have less time to lock arms with our teammates and play in the unique game God has called us to.

Looking back on my life, the victories that stand out have little to do with the large events. Those, as it turns out, were fleeting moments. Instead, my mind goes back to settings like the one on the basketball court in the Philippines. It's stories of developing my teammates into people who reached their full potential. People I didn't shy away from having hard conversations with. Even when I wanted to. People who may have never found fulfillment in their own personal mission if not given the chance to first play on my team.

14. PLAY OUTSIDE

In this final chapter, I'm going to end with a fun story. It's not a story of inspiration as much as it is a story of enticement. In the same way that parents all across this country are prying phones from their kids clutches and luring them to a fuller experience outside their front door, I too want to entice you to a life outside. It's only outside that adventures are lived and new stories are created. Stories, like the one I'm about to tell, remind us of how life is one big opportunity ready for the taking. Stories that take on a life of their own and are retold at every reunion for the rest of your life. In addition to the enticement that this story provides, I believe there are also four concluding lessons we can apply. Lessons from that time when I won the hottest and most elusive ticket in the world.

J is a friend of mine. I've only known him as an adult, but it's not hard to picture J as a ten-year-old neighbor coming over day after day and asking my mother if I can come out and play. J is an instigator. He is an optimist with a voracious appetite for more: more excitement, more opportunities, more relationships. Just more of everything. That characteristic alone isn't what makes him so unique. Lots of people want more, but J is willing to work for it. He has old-school ambition and enough experience to know that if he wants something, he has to go out and get it.

Observing J's lifestyle throughout our friendship has inspired me. He has helped me understand that in order to carry out our God-given dreams from Part 1. We need initiative. I have lots of stories of all the ways I've witnessed J's initiative over the years, but there is one adventure that stands out. It has everything a good story needs: a bit of embarrassment, a fair amount of luck, and a whole lot of risk.

J understands that good things come to those who wait; he just believes that better things come to those who knock on doors. Doors of opportunity and doors of invitation. I'm grateful that I was one of those doors, and I'm even more grateful that when he asked me to come outside to play, I had the courage to say yes.

Lesson 1: Say Yes

In January 2000, J's favorite football team, the Tennessee Titans, made it to the Super Bowl. J understood that this might be a once-in-a-lifetime event, and there was no way he would be content to sit on a couch and watch it from the confines of his living room. He had to make a road trip out of it. Whatever it took, he was determined to watch the game in person. J wanted more than just a closer seat; he wanted to participate and contribute in some small way.

J had no tickets, mind you, but that didn't deter him. About a week prior to the game, he asked if I would join him on a ten-hour road trip to Atlanta, home of the 2000 Super Bowl. His initial plan was to arrive in Atlanta during Super Bowl week, take in the sights, and drive back home in time to watch the game. It sounded like a respectable plan, but this wasn't my first adventure with J. I knew he wanted more. And to be honest, I did too. I think we both understood that a sound and safe plan was what we needed to get us out the door while maintaining some level of support from our wives.

The game was on a Sunday, and the soonest I could leave was after a campus ministry meeting on Wednesday night. We never even considered leaving Thursday morning. He arrived at my house about 10:00 p.m. Wednesday night bursting with optimism and excitement. Let's just say that he definitely brought my friend Anticipation with him! J was giddy like a kid, and I was thoroughly entertained by his excitement.

As we pulled out of my driveway, he mentioned that he'd seen something on television about an hour earlier that had him amped up—something about free Super Bowl tickets. But it wasn't until we were driving through the middle of Tennessee around 4:00 a.m. that I got the full story.

Apparently, a group of people sponsored by Jose Cuervo Tequila were randomly giving away Super Bowl tickets. Of course, J was convinced that we were going to win those free tickets, and I was amazed at his unwavering optimism. Even though I knew about some of his previous crazy adventures, I chalked them up to luck. But now that I was in the whirlwind with him, I started to see how he made his own luck. Like the time he won a $5,000 prize at a leadership convention with over 4,000 attendees. It was between sessions when a hype man came up on stage and took people through a series of questions that built up their confidence to participate. While everyone else was busy raising their hands, J was already walking in a beeline to the stage. He understood where this promotion was going before the other 4,000 people did, and it was J's combination of intelligence and initiative that got him on that stage as a finalist.

Now that I was in J's world, I was experiencing the optimism he always embodied. *So, this is what it feels like to be J,* I thought. It was different and a little scary, but I felt so alive! Rationally, I had zero belief that we would get free Super Bowl tickets, but emotionally, it felt good to hope. As we drove through the night, we swapped what-if scenarios, and we kept each other awake with optimism and caffeine. However, by the time we hit the Atlanta city limits around 9:00 a.m., our optimism was beginning to wear off. We were tired and hungry, not to mention unshowered. There were no hotels available, and this adventure was beginning to feel like one big mistake.

We had no place to be, no GPS to get there, and all the time in the world. Consequently, we found ourselves driving aimlessly around the city. That's when our adrenalin gave out and the emotional hangover kicked in. *I mean, what was J thinking? And why did I agree to this?* We didn't know what else to do, so we parked the car and started walking around. We were so tired.

We hadn't walked very far when J blurted out, "Hey, there's Big Dawg!" I knew exactly who he was referring to. As huge NFL fans, both

J and I had an appreciation for other teams as well as our own. Big Dawg was a superfan of the Cleveland Browns. He's a rather large person who wears a dog mask in the Cleveland endzone (named the Dawg Pound). The Browns were not in the Super Bowl that year, so it was a bit odd to see him in Atlanta. Clearly, he was being used as a promoter. We were intrigued and walked toward him. This wasn't exactly the incredible story I was hoping for, but I reasoned that meeting a superfan was better than nothing.

As we got closer, we started to see other superfans—from Green Bay, Minnesota, and Chicago—milling about. *What was this?* Then J said, "Dude, these are the people giving away free tickets!" I rolled my eyes, certain that J was joking, but as I focused on what each of the superfans were wearing, it was clear that they were sponsored by something. Jose Cuervo! These were the people!

I turned to give J a high five, but he was already approaching some official looking men in suits. I overheard him explaining our story. "We saw you on ESPN last night, and we just drove through the night to find you!" J's optimism was so strong and his power of persuasion so effective, they didn't appear to have any choice but to give us some tickets.

Turns out, however, that these tickets were not exactly free. They said we needed to show our fanaticism in some way. My mind was racing because I hate being put on the spot. What could I do to prove I was a fanatic? I looked into Big Dawg's eyes, desperate for some help. He instantly proposed that I get a crazy haircut. A mohawk seemed too routine, so he suggested a reverse mohawk, where I'd be shaved bald right down the center of my head. This was a good start, but I could tell they wanted more.

J and I were both feeling the mounting pressure of coming up with something significantly crazy to do before they turned their attention elsewhere. I was at a loss. Big Dawg's counterpart, the Bone Lady, was quick to come to my rescue. She, too, was a superfan of the Cleveland Browns and wore big glasses, a gaudy brown-and-orange skirt, and a Pebbles-like bone in her beehive hairdo. When she sensed my uncertainty, she suggested I put on her fishnet stockings while running around the CNN Center and screaming that I'd just won Super Bowl tickets. This seemed to be enough to appease the ticket-giving gods. *Whew!* I was in!

Now, as you might imagine, J was more comfortable reacting on the spot. He decided to be a bit more fanatical by eating a $100 bill. But not just any $100 bill—*my* $100 bill. Considering that tickets were going for more than $1,000, I didn't mind. This was a bargain, and all he had to do was swallow some paper. It sounded easy enough, but it turns out that saliva has no effect on breaking down paper money. He was chewing and chewing, desperate to get it down, but all to no avail. Desperate, he ended up tearing it into three pieces, and with the help of lots of water, he finally choked it down. We did it! We were going to the Super Bowl!

Suddenly, we were surrounded by cameras, being interviewed by CNN, ABC, CBS, and ESPN. All of them were asking us about our superfan plan, but we didn't even know where we'd be sleeping the next few nights. Not that we were worried about it. I mean, if we could get free Super Bowl tickets, finding some housing shouldn't be a problem, right? And it wasn't. Two of the superfans quickly came to our aid. They each had an extra bed available in their hotel room, and we were readily adopted into this exclusive family of fanatic fans. We offered Green Bay's Title Town Clown and his Minnesota Viking counterpart six-packs as a token of our appreciation. And just like that, we had a place to stay, a community that welcomed us, and the hottest tickets in the world.

Sometimes the greatest opportunities actually do come to your front door. The question is, when they do, will you pull out the list of reasons it doesn't make sense right now or recognize that right now is the perfect time to utter the word that starts all great adventures . . . "yes."

Lesson 2. Take a Risk

As I lied in bed that first night. I kept pinching myself, wondering if this was real. It is a rare and wonderful feeling to bask in the rewards of taking a risk. A feeling I wanted more of. It was a feeling of peace, excitement, and anticipation all rolled into one. It was like I was a kid again! I knew the sweetness of this moment would eventually wear off, so as I drifted off to sleep, I soaked in all the positive feelings I could. I didn't want to forget that my life was meant to be lived in the realm of adventure. I especially didn't want to forget that the key to that realm was risk. And what exactly did we risk? Three days of discomfort and a little gas money? Our worst-case scenario was getting bored and driving home with fewer dollars than before. Saying it like that makes me wonder why more people didn't make the trip. I guess we were just willing to try something no one else was willing to try. Perhaps it's because most people like the idea of trying more than trying itself. And it probably won't surprise you when I say that the same dynamic is at play when it comes to pursuing our personal mission.

Unfortunately, many of us have eliminated the word "try" from our Christian context. Instead, we equate the Christian life with a safe, stable, and, ultimately, idle life. What was meant to be a life of following Jesus on a spiritual adventure has been reduced to believing a few theological statements. As a result, we think that Christianity is something to be believed but not lived. However, there's a question we have to ask ourselves: Is Jesus more interested in what we think about our faith or in what we do with our faith? Merely thinking doesn't get things done, nor does it advance the kingdom. That's why the first step to making a difference starts by walking out the front door and playing outside. Do you want to understand the needs at your elementary school? Volunteer as a lunch aid. Do you want more for your neighborhood? Throw a block party. Do you want to get what others don't have? Then you will need to take risks that others don't. Risks that lead you not only to the heights of free Super Bowl tickets but also to outcomes that you could have never seen coming.

Lesson 3: Welcome Surprises

Leading a life of playful experimentation will inevitably lead us to a few surprises. It's in these moments that we need to lean in and embrace the new relationship, new opportunity, or even new obstacle with optimism. This is the discipline I most admire in others. And with J by my side, I was about to embrace a surprise so big that it would become the thing I remembered and retold more than the game itself. Here is the rest of the story.

A couple days into our stay, J invited me to his room. He said he had something significant to show me. He was tentative and struggled to find the right words. This was unlike J, so I patiently waited. Eventually, he just pointed to the sink. As I approached, I saw three pieces of paper soaking in standing water. Could this be . . . ? *Oh, my.* Yes, these were the same three pieces he'd ingested a couple days before. Somehow, J had found the courage to sift through his own sewage to reclaim the $100 bill he had eaten on that dare!

Uncertain how to proceed, we stared silently at the discolored remnants. Our first idea was to put them in a small plastic bag and take them to the bank. However, when we did, the teller just looked at us and said, "That's not money." Then we went back to the hotel, brainstormed for a while, and eventually decided to tape the pieces back together and use the bill to pay for breakfast at Shoney's. It worked! (Perhaps now is a good time to affirm that our mothers were right when they told us, "You don't know where that money has been!")

It's interesting to me that something as inconspicuous as our method of payment for the grandest event on the planet quickly turned into the main story. And the same thing can happen when you begin to experiment with pursuing your mission. What you currently believe to be your grand mission may be full of surprises that lead you to something else—maybe something more helpful or more memorable.

So, what apparent distractions are you currently experiencing? Could it be that these smaller stories are actually the main point? For example, have you put your personal mission toward your neighborhood on hold because it's a busy season at work? Maybe it's because your workplace is emerging as a grander mission for this particular season. Are you frustrated that the same person keeps interfering with your attempts to help your family member? Maybe it's the person who appears to be "in the way" that needs your help the most.

It's amazing how the stories that surprise us often become the grandest. Indeed, they may come out of left field, but they don't come to our couch. We have to get out of the house. We have to take some risks. It's only then that we will give God a chance to bless us with a different story that will drown out everything else—even a ticket to the Super Bowl.

Lesson 4. Stay Outside

It feels appropriate to end this book where it started—in the parking lot of an amusement park. That same park where my preteen friends showed me the power of permission. You may not fully understand it, but like an eighth-grade kid, it's your turn to enter this new world of possibilities waiting for you on the other side of those turnstiles.

Can you feel the rush of uncertainty? Is the thrill of anticipation by your side? Or do you feel skeptical, scared, or indifferent? Whenever we find ourselves on the threshold of a new adventure, we have a choice. We can get back on the bus where everything is predictable and familiar, or we can take the risk of embracing the unknown. It's in moments like these that we need friends willing to grab us by the shirt collar, look us in the eyes, and passionately remind us that we have permission to live boldly. If you'll allow me, I'd like to now be that friend to you.

"Yes, it is true, you are a person full of flaws and failures. You may be inexperienced, tired, or bored. It's likely that you are busy and distracted, even skeptical and scared, but you are God's best choice. He longs to lock arms with you. He wants you on his team. He has experiences and gifts for you that you could never receive back on the bus. Look around. All you need to do is take a few more steps.

"You have permission."

ACKNOWLEDGEMENTS

Jesus:

I don't know why you have blessed me with the life I get to live. You have shown me more than I can imagine. Taught me more than I can remember. Blessed me more than I deserve. Thank you.

Paulette:

Your unwavering belief in me has been my source of stability over the years. The hundreds of hours we've spent in conversation on a bar stool on date night has brought me more peace and confidence than all the other voices combined. Thank you.

Mattea, Kordell, Judah, Wren, and Josh:

I'm proud to be your dad. You've all given me such incredible encouragement. Your sincere and ongoing support has not gone unnoticed. Each of you have patiently listened and contributed to my readings, my writings, and my ramblings. Thank you.

Micah:

I'm proud to be your dad as well. You embody the "personal mission" I so desperately want the world to know. You beautifully leverage your unique talent to enrich the world and the people in it. You were the perfect person to designed the cover of this book. Thank you.

Brian Sanders, Neil Cole, Sam Metcalf, Alan Hirsch, Rich Robinson, JR Woodward:

Your writings have opened my eyes to a world I can't unsee. Thank you.

My supporters:

It's because of you that I get to live out a mission that few others can. I don't take lightly that my unique opportunities for kingdom advancement come at the sacrifice of those who stand with me. I couldn't do this without you. Thank you.

My alumni:

You are my heroes. You are the ones that have shown me that in the midst of changing diapers, engine oil, and careers, your personal mission can still thrive. May God bless you.

ABOUT THE AUTHOR

PETE has a long history with launching people into personal missions from the college campus. He has been a pioneer coach to multiple ministries and organizations in over 10 countries. In addition to serving on an international steering committee, he also established campus ministries of his own in Hungary, China and the Philippines. Pete and his wife Paulette spent the majority of their ministry life at Illinois State University. It's here that he served as the campus minister for 22 years and together with his wife raised 5 kids. Pete now resides just outside of Raleigh North Carolina. He is the founder of Per Mission Inc and has helped create a network for spiritual entrepreneurs called the Diffuse Network. He loves all sports and enjoys long talks with the dreamers of the world. Also, it should be noted that he exercises just enough to keep from being embarrassed by his tri-athlete wife.